Knitting

FOR

DUMMIES®

POCKET EDITION

by Pam Allen, Tracy L. Barr,
and Shannon Okey

WILEY

John Wiley & Sons, Inc.

Knitting For Dummies® Pocket Edition

Published by
John Wiley & Sons, Inc.
111 River St.
Hoboken, NJ 07030-5774
www.wiley.com

For general information on our other products and services, please contact our Customer Care Department within the U.S. at 877-762-2974, outside the U.S. at 317-572-3993, or fax 317-572-4002.

For technical support, please visit www.wiley.com/techsupport.

Wiley publishes in a variety of print and electronic formats and by print-on-demand. Some material included with standard print versions of this book may not be included in e-books or in print-on-demand. If this book refers to media such as a CD or DVD that is not included in the version you purchased, you may download this material at http://booksupport.wiley.com. For more information about Wiley products, visit www.wiley.com.

Library of Congress Control Number is available from the publisher.

ISBN 978-1-118-30683-3 (pbk); ISBN 978-1-118-30684-0 (ebk); ISBN 978-1-118-30685-7 (ebk); ISBN 978-1-118-30687-1 (ebk)

Manufactured in the United States of America

10 9 8 7 6 5 4 3 2 1

Publisher's Acknowledgments

Project Editor: Elizabeth Kuball
Composition Services: Indianapolis Composition Services Department
Cover Photo: © iStockphoto.com / James Richey

Table of Contents

Introduction

• •

*S*everal years ago, a major New York City department store ran a humorous ad disparaging knitting as an activity for grandmothers. The response?
Ardent members of New York's Big Apple Knitting
Guild took up their yarn and needles and staged a
knit-in. To demonstrate that knitting isn't an activity
limited to the rocking chair set but rather is an alive
and timely art, a group of knitters of every age and
gender gathered in the store to spend the afternoon
knitting. Designer and knitter par excellence Lily Chin
designed, knit, and wore a shimmering slit-to-the-
thigh floor-length gown — demonstrating that more
than button-to-the-throat cardigans and stiff socks
can come off the needles.

Sure, grandmothers knit, but so do movie stars, foot-
ball players, doctors, and lawyers. They know what
all knitters know or find out soon after getting into the
groove of knitting: that knitting does more than just
provide you with warm and cozy things to wear.
Knitting stirs creativity, gives you an ongoing sense of
purpose, teaches patience, and soothes the soul.
Don't believe me? Try it!

Now is a great time to learn to knit. Never before have
knitters had so many lovely and imaginative yarns
from which to choose and so many stylish and
sophisticated patterns to work with.

About This Book

The purpose of *Knitting For Dummies,* Pocket Edition, is to put all the need-to-know information about knitting into one easy-to-read and easy-to-follow book. Although you can jump in anywhere you find a topic that interests you, the overall organization of this book progresses from basic to more advanced skills. To that end, each chapter is divided into sections, and each section contains important skill-building information about knitting, such as

✔ How to cast on, and which of the different cast-on techniques are better for particular purposes

✔ How to read pattern instructions

✔ How to combine knit and purl stitches for different effects

✔ What to do if you drop a stitch or inadvertently add one

In addition, you'll find projects that enable you to practice and perfect your skills.

Conventions Used in This Book

To help you navigate through this book and easily follow the project and pattern instructions, we've set up a few conventions:

✔ General processes are presented in step format, where the main instruction appears in **boldface** and any explanatory information appears in regular type below it.

- ✔ Knitting instructions appear in the format common to many knitting books, using common abbreviations. For an explanation of the abbreviations, turn to Chapter 3.

- ✔ To indicate the needle you carry in your left hand, we use the abbreviation LH. To indicate the needle in your right hand (the one on which you make stitches), we use RH.

- ✔ Most patterns in this book call for worsted-weight yarn (exceptions are noted). Because companies frequently change their yarn lineups from season to season, you may not be able to find the exact yarn or colorway shown in a book pattern in your local yarn store, and that's okay. You can substitute almost any other worsted-weight yarn in the patterns shown in this book that list it in the directions. Some reliable choices are Cascade 220, Brown Sheep Lamb's Pride, Lion Wool, Plymouth Galway, and Louet Gems Worsted. You can also run a search for yarns by weight on `www.yarndex.com`, an online database for finding yarns that meet certain criteria such as weight, fiber content, or color. Or ask the friendly staff at your local yarn store for help in finding the right yarn!

- ✔ `Monofont` is the typeface we use for web addresses. When this book was printed, some web addresses may have needed to break across two lines of text. If that happened, rest assured that we haven't put in any extra characters (such as hyphens) to indicate the break. So, when using one of these web addresses, just type in exactly what you see in this book, pretending as though the line break doesn't exist.

Icons Used in This Book

Throughout this book, we use icons to highlight important information.

This icon lets you in on some secrets most knitters learn from one another. It also indicates special ways to make your project just a little bit better. You can get by without applying this info, but if you do take our advice, your project will be that much nicer.

If you see this icon, we're pointing out hazards on the knitting path. Pay attention to these if you don't want to find yourself in tangles.

This icon alerts you to something you probably already know and that you'll need to remember and apply in the project at hand or in other projects down the road.

Where to Go from Here

You've got your copy of *Knitting For Dummies,* Pocket Edition — now what? If you're looking to stock up on the tools you need, turn to Chapter 2. If you want to learn the basic stitches you'll use for years to come, turn to Chapter 5. And if you want to dive into making something you can use, turn to Chapter 9.

If you want even more patterns and knitting tips, check out the full-size version of *Knitting For Dummies,* 2nd Edition — simply head to your local book seller or go to www.dummies.com!

Chapter 1

Two Needles, a Ball of Yarn, and a Little Know-how

. . . .

In This Chapter

▶ Exploring the many reasons to knit

▶ Collecting tips for how to best learn knitting from a book

. . . .

Knitting is a relatively simple process requiring minimal tools — two needles and a ball of yarn. Its basic structure of interlocking loops couldn't be less complicated. Yet the possibilities for design and pattern innovation are endless. Knitting has more than cozy socks and colorful sweaters to offer; it's also an excellent way to mitigate some of the stresses and frustrations of day-to-day life.

This chapter introduces you to knitting — what it is and what it takes, why it's so darn good for you, and how to best go about learning to knit from a book. With the info you find in this chapter and the skills you pick up in the others, you'll be able to explore with confidence the myriad things you can do with two needles and a ball of yarn.

Why Knit?

Knitting's been around for hundreds of years, and for a large portion of that time, it was a utilitarian endeavor. But chances are, you're not taking up knitting because you need to restock your sock drawer or whip up much needed sweaters and scarves to keep out the winter chill. So, why knit?

Knitting up good karma

Ask knitters why they knit and you'll get a variety of answers. But the one you'll hear from nearly every knitter, regardless of the other reasons they may give, is "It's relaxing."

The repetitive movements of needles and yarn truly knit up the raveled sleeve of care. Have you ever noticed a knitter's face while working away on the needles? Did you see the expression of relaxed alertness? The rhythmic movements of knitting, together with the mental focus needed for building fabric stitch by stitch, make for a kind of meditation. It's real. Ask anyone who knits.

And if you carry your knitting wherever you go, you always bring along a little well-being with you. In an increasingly global and anonymous world, a knitting project at hand reminds you of the comforts and familiarity of things small, local, and individual.

A feeling of accomplishment

A skein of yarn can be anything, but it's nothing — despite how beautiful the color or how soft the feel — until someone gives it shape and purpose. So, when you knit, you use your skill, your imagination, your patience, and your perseverance to create something from nothing.

Turning skeins of yarn, stitch by stitch, into hats, afghans, socks, bags, sweaters, cardigans, and more gives you a feeling of competence and accomplishment that few other hobbies can offer. And it's a sense that grows with each row, with each wearing, with each "Oooh, it's so beautiful (or warm, or soft)" comment that you hear.

Keeping your mind and hands occupied

If you knit a little while waiting for your computer to load screens, red lights to turn green, and commercials to end, you'll never have to worry about wasting time again.

Knitting is portable, too, so you can work on your project wherever you find yourself. You can knit in the living room while you're watching TV or in the kitchen while waiting for the pasta to cook. You can knit while waiting to catch a plane or while sitting on a park bench watching your children play. You can take your knitting with you, whether it's a challenging project that requires quiet concentration or something simple that you can tote along and pull out at the odd moment for a quick row or two.

Studies have shown that hobbies like knitting can even be good for your waistline. How? Because it's really hard to snack while watching TV if your hands are busy.

Creating a one-of-a-kind piece

Knitting is a process of combining yarn, needles, pattern, and color. Even if all you do is follow a sweater pattern by using the exact yarn and needles it calls for, each stitch is of your own making, and no two sweaters from the same pattern worked by different knitters are ever exactly the same.

After your first project or two, there's a good chance that you'll be venturing with pleasure into the wonderland of new combinations of yarn, pattern stitch, color, and embellishment. You'll be wondering how you'll ever find the time to make all the ideas in your head a reality.

Creativity is less about being born with a friendly muse and more about putting time and effort into developing know-how. Granted, moments of inspiration *can* wake you up at 4 o'clock in the morning, but rarely do they happen unless you first lay the groundwork. Work all day on finding the right color combination for a project, and the solution will come at an unlikely moment. By learning, practicing, and mastering your art and craft, you become creative.

Teaching Yourself to Knit from a Book

Everyone learns a new skill in a different way. If you're not confident that you can teach yourself to knit from a book, you can do the following things to make the process easier and help to ensure success:

✔ **Study the illustrations carefully and compare them with what your own hands, needles, and yarn are doing.**

✔ **Use your right hand (not your left) if a right hand is pictured.**

✔ **Notice the path of the yarn in the illustration and see whether yours is doing the same thing.** For example, does the yarn cross from right to left, or over or under the needle?

✔ **Keep a pad of sticky notes nearby and use them on the book pages to help you focus on the illustration or text you're trying to understand.**

✔ **If you get stuck, gather your materials and head to your local knitting shop.** Most store personnel are happy to help a new knitter get up and running. While you're there, ask whether the store sponsors a knitting group or knows of any that meet in your area. You can learn loads from other knitters. Or sign up for a knitting list on the web, and you won't have to leave home. Whatever you do, don't give up. The rewards of being a knitter are worth the effort of learning how to be one.

Swatching

Swatching (making a sample of knitted fabric) is to the knitter what scales and exercises are to the pianist and what rough sketches and doodles are to the painter. A swatch is a sample of knitting. It can be big (50 stitches and 50 rows) or small (20 stitches and 20 rows). Most of the time, knitters make a swatch to measure gauge (to see how many stitches and rows there are to an inch). But dedicated knitters also work up swatches to learn, to practice, to experiment, and to invent.

Your swatch can tell you

- Whether your yarn and needles work up to the necessary gauge
- Whether your yarn shows off your stitch pattern or obscures it
- Whether your chosen color combination works or needs tweaking
- Whether you understand a new technique

As you go through or skip around this book, we urge you to keep your yarn and needles handy to try out the patterns, stitches, and techniques given. In some cases, we even provide specific instructions in the project sections for making a sampler of a particular technique.

The swatches you make will keep you limber, stretch your knowledge, and be your best teacher.

Putting it into practice

This book provides projects to allow you to practice the skills introduced. Pick a few of these to knit up. Although swatches are invaluable when you want to practice a particular technique, there's nothing like an actual project to let you practice multiple techniques at one time. By making real things, your knowledge and confidence grow immeasurably — even if what you initially end up with are things that you wouldn't want anyone else to see!

Whatever you do, don't give up. Before you know it, you'll be wearing your knitted pieces out in public or giving them as gifts to family and friends. And when people inquire, "Did you *make* this?" you'll be able to proudly answer, "Yes, I did!"

Chapter 2

Tools of the Trade

● ●

In This Chapter

▶ Understanding your yarn options

▶ Choosing knitting needles

▶ Selecting the right gadgets for even better results

● ●

*T*ruth be told, you can spend quite a few hours happily knitting away with nothing more than some spare yarn and an old pair of knitting needles. If you take to knitting, however, your satisfaction with these basic supplies will soon morph into a desire to experiment with the array of beautiful yarns and designer needles that are available.

With so many choices in stores and online, choosing the yarns and needles that are right for you — or the project you have in mind — can be a bit daunting. This chapter's here to help. It gives you the lowdown on different kinds of yarns and needles and explains how to pick the right tools for your projects.

Yarn: The (Quick) Consumer's Guide

A nice yarn shop is a knitter's paradise. Heck, even the yarn section of a discount or craft store can be a little slice of heaven. Why? Because of all the traditional and specialty yarns that are available. With such an abundance of choices, how do you decide what yarn to buy? Knowing a little bit about the different types of yarn and their general characteristics helps. So, first things first.

Yarn is made from short fibers that come from animals or plants or are synthetic. The fibers are combed, or *carded,* to align them into a soft untwisted rope (called *roving*). Then they're spun (twisted) into a strand or ply of yarn. This single ply is usually combined with other plies to form the final yarn.

The following sections explain the two main factors — fiber and weight — that account for the wide variety of yarns available. Whether you prefer your yarn plain or fancy, some knowledge of yarn basics can ensure that what looks great on the shelf will look great in your finished project, too.

Fiber fundamentals

All yarn is made from natural or synthetic fibers. Different fibers have different qualities — some good, some not so good. Often, to offset an undesirable characteristic, yarn manufacturers combine different fibers. (A *blend* is a yarn made from fibers of different origins — for example, wool/cotton, wool/silk, alpaca/cotton.) More than anything else, the combination of fibers in your yarn determines its ultimate look, feel, and wearable comfort.

Yarn consists of one or more strands called *plies*. Plied yarns are made from two, three, or four plies of yarn twisted together. Multi-plied and firmly twisted yarns are usually strong, smooth, and even. Lightly twisted plied and single-ply yarns are closer to their roving (unspun) state and, though sturdy enough when knitted up, can pull apart into strands if they're over-handled. They also can be slightly uneven, have more loft and softness, and be warmer than their twisted sisters.

A fabric's *hand* is how it feels to the touch. Just as pieces of woven fabric from silk or wool differ in *drape* (how it falls) and softness, so do knits from different fibers. But fiber isn't all that accounts for drape and softness. The size of the needle you use with a given yarn affects the feel of your knitted piece. The larger the needle and looser the stitch, the softer and drapier the fabric. The smaller the needle and tighter the stitch, the stiffer the fabric.

Wool and other fleece yarns

Wool (made from the fleece of sheep) is the queen of yarns, and it endures and remains a popular choice for knitters for a number of excellent reasons.

Wool is a good insulator — warm in winter, cool in summer. It can absorb lots of moisture without feeling wet, and it absorbs dye beautifully. It's resilient — the fibers can stretch and bend repeatedly but always return to their original shape. It's soft, relatively light-weight, and beautiful to look at. And, key to beginning knitters, wool is easy to knit with because it has just enough give. It also can be pulled out and reknit easily, a bonus when you're just learning the basic stitches.

Although all wool yarns are wonderful to work with, they vary tremendously depending on the breed of sheep or combination of breeds they come from, how they're spun, whether they're plied or single stranded, and whether they're treated for washability or not.

Silk, cotton, linen, and rayon

Silk, cotton, linen, and rayon yarns are the slippery yarns. Unlike rough yarns from the hairy fibers of animals, their smooth and often shiny surfaces cause them to unravel quickly if you drop a stitch. These yarns are inelastic and may stretch lengthwise over time. Often, they're blended with other fibers (natural and synthetic) to counteract their disadvantages. But silk and cotton, even in their pure state, are so lovely to look at and comfortable to wear that they're well worth knitting.

Synthetic yarns

Originally, synthetics (nylon, acrylic, and polyester) were made to mimic the look and feel of natural materials. Knitters give mixed reviews to 100-percent synthetic yarns.

- ✔ **On the plus side:** All-synthetic yarns are inexpensive and hold up well in the washing machine. For people who are allergic to wool, synthetics make for a look-alike substitute (at least from a distance).

- ✔ **On the downside:** All-synthetic yarns don't have the wonderful insulating and moisture-absorbing qualities of natural yarns and therefore can be uncomfortable to wear. For the same reason, they can make your hands clammy when you're knitting. They pill more readily than wool or other fibers, and once exposed to heat (a hot iron is deadly), they lose all resilience and become flat.

These complaints and synthetic yarns' dubious reputation have encouraged manufacturers to come up with new and better applications for synthetics. Perhaps the best use for synthetic yarns is in combination with other fibers. Manufacturers now engineer blended yarns for certain qualities. For example, nylon is extremely strong and light, and it adds durability when blended in small amounts with more fragile fibers such as mohair. A little nylon blended with wool makes a superb sock yarn. A little acrylic in cotton makes the yarn lighter and pro-motes *memory* (so that the knitted fabric doesn't stretch out of shape).

Novelty yarns

Novelty yarns are easy to recognize because their appearance is so different from traditional yarns. Their jewel colors and whimsical textures can be hard to resist. Following are some of the more common novelty, or specialty, yarns you'll come across:

- **Ribbon:** This is usually a knitted ribbon in rayon or a rayon blend with wonderful drape.

- **Boucle:** This highly bumpy, textured yarn is comprised of loops.

- **Chenille:** Although tricky to knit with, the attractive appearance and velvety texture of this yarn make your perseverance worthwhile.

- **Thick-thin:** Often handspun, these yarns alter-nate between very thick and thin sections, which lends a charmingly bumpy look to knitted fabric.

- **Railroad ribbon:** This ribbon-style yarn has tiny "tracks" of fiber strung between two parallel strands of thread.

- **Faux fur:** Fluffy fiber strands on a strong base thread of nylon resemble faux fur when knitted.

✔ **"Traditional" novelty yarns:** Tweeds, heathered, marled, and handpainted yarns all create more subtle effects than modern novelty yarns do and can add lovely variety to your knitting basket.

- **Tweed:** Usually wool, this yarn has a background color flecked with bits of fiber in different colors.

- **Heather:** This yarn has been blended from a number of different-colored or dyed fleeces, and then spun. Heather yarns are muted in color; think of them as the yarn equivalent of watercolors.

- **Marled (ragg) yarn:** This is a plied yarn in which the plies are different colors.

- **Variegated yarn:** This yarn is dyed in several different colors or shades of a single color. Hand-dyed yarn (often called *handpainted*) is very popular and knits up in a series of random color repeats that would be difficult to imitate using even a large number of different-colored yarns.

A weighty matter

Yarns come in different *weights,* or thicknesses. The weight of your yarn (among other things) has a huge impact on the look of your final product and certainly the amount of time it takes to knit it up.

The weight of a yarn determines how many stitches it takes to knit 1 inch. A medium-weight yarn that knits up 5 stitches and 7 rows to the inch takes 35 stitches to make a square inch of knitted fabric. A bulky yarn at 3 stitches and 5 rows to the inch needs 15 stitches to make a square inch. You can see the difference in Figure 2-1.

Although there are no official categories for yarn weights, many knitting books and yarn manufacturers use common terms to indicate a yarn's thickness and the size needle the yarn is usually worked on. Table 2-1 lists these categories for you.

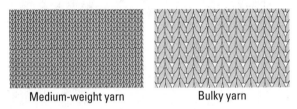

Medium-weight yarn   Bulky yarn

Figure 2-1: Different weights create different effects.

Table 2-1		Common Yarn Weights	
Yarn Weight	*US Needle Size*	*Stitches Per Inch*	*Common Uses*
Lace	000–1	8–10	Lace knitting
Super fine, fingering, or baby-weight	1–3	7–8	Light layettes, socks
Fine or sport-weight	3–6	5–6	Light sweaters, baby things, accessories
Light worsted or DK (double-knitting)	5–7	5–5½	Sweaters and other garments, light-weight scarves
Medium- or worsted-weight, afghan, Aran	7–9	4–5	Sweaters, blankets, outdoor wear (hats, scarves, mittens, and so on)

(continued)

Table 2-1 *(continued)*

Yarn Weight	US Needle Size	Stitches Per Inch	Common Uses
Bulky or chunky	10–11	3–3½	Rugs, jackets, blankets
Super Bulky	13–15	2–2½	Heavy blankets and rugs, although a trend towards using this yarn weight for sweaters has been underway for some time now

The thickness of a given yarn is determined by the individual thickness of the plies, *not* by the number of plies. If the plies are thin, a 4-ply yarn can be finer than a heavy single-ply yarn.

Looking at yarn packaging

Yarn is packaged in different ways — balls, skeins (rhymes with *canes*), and hanks (see Figure 2-2). Balls and skeins come ready to knit. When you find the end, you can cast on and go. Hanks need to be wound into a ball before you can use them. If you try to knit with the yarn in hank form, you'll quickly end up with a tangled mess.

Your local yarn store may offer a winding service to convert hanks of yarn to center-pull balls using a yarn *winder* and a *swift* — two pieces of equipment that allow you to make an easy-to-use "cake" of yarn that sits flat as you knit it.

If at all possible, you want to start knitting with the yarn end that comes from the *inside* of the skein or ball. This way the skein or ball will remain in place as you knit and not roll around the floor attracting the attention of a cat (or other pet) on attack. If you're lucky, the inside end will already be pulled to the outside — ready to go. If not, you have to reach in and pull out a small hunk of yarn in order to find this end and then rewrap the extra.

Each ball, skein, or hank comes wrapped with a label (see Figure 2-3) that you should read carefully. It gives you useful information and lets you know whether the yarn is a good candidate for the project you have in mind. If the yarn begs to be purchased before you know what you want to make with it, the information on the label will let you know what kind of project best suits it.

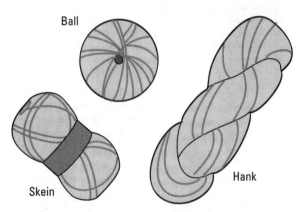

Ball

Hank

Skein

Figure 2-2: Yarn comes in balls, skeins, and hanks.

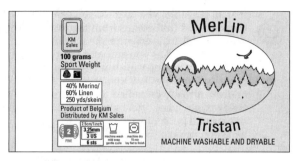

Figure 2-3: A sample yarn label.

On the yarn label, pay particular attention to

- ✔ **Gauge (how many stitches and rows per inch) and suggested needle size:** This information gives you an idea of what the final knitted fabric will look like. A size US 11 (7½ mm) needle and a gauge of low numbers (3 stitches and 5 rows per 1 inch) will yield a heavy, chunky fabric. A size US 5 (3¾ mm) needle and a gauge of 5 stitches and 7 rows per 1 inch will yield a finer, more traditional fabric.

- ✔ **Fiber content:** This lets you know whether the yarn is wool, cotton, acrylic, a blend, or something else. If you intend to make a washable garment, check to see whether the yarn is machine- or hand-washable or strictly a dry-clean fiber.

- ✔ **Dye lot number and/or color number:** This information indicates what batch of dye this yarn came from. When you buy multiple skeins of yarn, compare these numbers to ensure that they're the same (that is, that all your yarn comes from the same dye batch). Even if you can't detect a difference in color between two balls of different dye lots, chances are the difference will become apparent when you knit them up one after the other.

Choosing yarn for a project

Yarns, garment shapes, and stitch patterns must work together for your project to be successful. With so many yarn choices available, how do you choose? If you plan to knit a scarf or a blanket — something for which sizing doesn't need to be precise — pick any yarn you take a fancy to and let its characteristics dictate the outcome of your project. If you're making a sweater (or anything else for which sizing is important) from a pattern, purchase the yarn the pattern specifies or one with a similar gauge to be a suitable substitute.

Matching the yarn to the stitch

The yarn you choose can either accentuate the effect you're trying to create or camouflage it. As a general rule, the wilder the yarn, the simpler the sweater shape and pattern stitch should be. The plainer the yarn, the more texture and shaping details will show up. Here are some guidelines:

✔ **Smooth-plied yarn in a solid color:** Use these yarns for cables and more complex stitch patterns. They give your stitches a crisp look, showcasing your effort. Cables and pattern stitches worked in soft single plies have a slightly softer appearance than when worked in highly twisted yarns. In general, plied and twisted yarns are sophisticated and classic. Single plies are rustic and relaxed. Smooth-plied yarns in contrasting colors are also good for

Fair Isle and intarsia patterns because they give you clear and readable patterns.

- ✔ **Variegated and novelty yarns:** Don't knock yourself out with tricky stitch work if you're using variegated or highly textured yarns. The stitches won't show up, and all your stitch-making effort will be for naught. Simple stitches, such as stockinette and garter, are best with these yarns.

- ✔ **For cotton, silk, soy, bamboo, and other inelastic yarns:** Look for patterns that don't depend on ribbing for fit. Find patterns that hang straight to highlight the drape of these yarns.

 If you shop in a specialty yarn store, chances are that the people who work there have experience with their yarns and with knitting in general. Feel free to ask questions about the yarn you're considering for your project. Here are some good ones to keep in mind:

- ✔ Does it pill?
- ✔ Is it colorfast?
- ✔ Will it stretch?
- ✔ Is it easy to knit with?
- ✔ Does it work with the pattern I've chosen?
- ✔ What size needle will it work best with?

Remember that your local yarn store (LYS, in online parlance) is an excellent resource for other knitting help, too. Sales associates can help you avoid many of the common pitfalls beginning knitters make in choosing yarn for projects.

 It isn't easy to predict what yarn in a ball will look like when it's knitted up. This is especially true of novelty yarns. Check to see whether the yarns you're interested in have been knitted into a sample. Many yarn shops knit up sample swatches or entire sweaters in the yarns they carry so that you can see what they look like worked up.

Substituting one yarn for another

Substituting one yarn for another can be tricky. It's not enough to pick a yarn that looks the same or that you like. You have to think of other things as well, including

✔ **Yardage:** Be sure to pay attention to actual yardage listed on the label, not just number of grams or ounces. A 50-gram, 1.75-ounce ball of yarn that's 148 yards isn't the same amount as a 50-gram, 1.75-ounce ball of yarn that's 126 yards.

✔ **Weight:** If you're substituting yarn, be sure the weight is the same. If the pattern you've chosen expects you to get 4 stitches and 6 rows to the inch and you substitute a yarn that gives you a different gauge, your sweater will turn out a different size than the one given in the pattern. (See the earlier section "A weighty matter" for general information on yarn weight and gauge; Chapter 3 explains how to measure gauge.)

✔ **Fiber:** Yarns of different fibers, even if they have the same gauge, will have different characteristics. Be sure you know the characteristics of the yarn and are comfortable with the way these differences will affect the finished piece. (The earlier section, "Fiber fundamentals," covers different kinds of yarn fibers and their characteristics.)

If you don't want to use or can't find the yarn specified in a pattern, the safest option — at least until you're experienced enough to take

into account all the factors that effect gauge, drape, and so on — is to talk to a sales associate in a specialty yarn shop. Chances are that anyone working in your local yarn shop is a knitter and can give you good advice based on experience. In a chain store, that may or may not be the case.

Just because two yarns have the same gauge doesn't mean that they can substitute for each other successfully in a given pattern. If they have different characteristics — texture, drape, fiber, and color — the final garment will look and feel different from the one pictured on your pattern.

Knitting Needles

Knitting needles come in a stunning assortment of materials, styles, and sizes to mesh with your knitting style, the particular project you're working on, your aesthetics, and your budget.

Exploring needles

You can choose from three kinds of knitting needles (see Figure 2-4):

✔ **Straight:** Straight needles are generally used for *flat knitting* — knitting on the right side, and then turning and knitting on the wrong side. Straight needles come in many standard lengths ranging from 7-inch "scarf needles" to those that are 10, 13, and 14 inches long. The larger your project, the longer the needle you'll need.

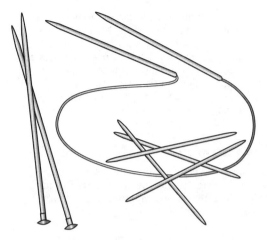

Figure 2-4: Three kinds of knitting needles.

- ✓ **Circular:** A circular needle is simply a pair of straight knitting needle tips joined by a flexible cable. You can use a circular needle to *knit in the round* — knitting in a continuous, spiral-like fashion without turning your work. This technique creates a seamless tube large enough for a sweater body or small enough for a neckband. You also can use a circular needle as you would straight needles, to work back and forth. This approach can be particularly handy for lengthwise-knit scarves, blankets, and other very wide pieces.

  Circular needles are available in many different lengths, most frequently 16, 24, 29, and 36 inches, although they're also available in sizes as long as 60 inches!

- ✓ **Double-pointed needles:** Double-pointed needles (abbreviated dpns) have a point at each end and are sold in sets of four or five needles. They work the same way as a circular needle — in rounds.

You use them to make small tubes when there are too few stitches to stretch around the circumference of a circular needle — for such things as sleeve cuffs, tops of hats, socks, mittens, and so on. They come in 7- and 10-inch lengths and recently have shown up in 5-inch lengths — a great boon to those who enjoy making socks and mittens.

Sizing them up

A needle's size is determined by its diameter. The smaller the size, the narrower the needle and the smaller the stitch it makes. Following are U.S. needle sizes and their metric equivalents:

U.S.	Metric
0	2 mm
1	2¼ mm
2	2¾ mm
3	3¼ mm
4	3½ mm
5	3¾ mm
6	4 mm
7	4½ mm
8	5 mm
9	5½ mm
10	6 mm
10½	6½ mm
11	8 mm
13	9 mm
15	10 mm

Gizmos and Gadgets

Lots of knitting gadgets are on the market. Some make life a little easier, and others are out-and-out lifesavers. Some you have to buy, but you can improvise others from what you already have on hand.

The essentials

For the most part, knitting gadgets are small and portable. Keep the essentials in a little zippered bag, and you can carry them anywhere your knitting goes.

Scissors

Small portable scissors are a must. In a pinch, you can break certain yarns with your hands, but others have to be cut with scissors. Collapsible scissors that fold up and don't leave any sharp points exposed are great. You can find them in most knitting stores.

Tape measure

A small retractable tape measure marked for inches and centimeters can go anywhere. Use it to measure your gauge swatch and to check your knitted pieces as you go along.

Tapestry needles

Tapestry needles, also called *yarn needles,* are simply large-eye needles with a blunt point that you use to sew knitted pieces together. When joining pieces of knitted fabric, you're working in the spaces around the stitches, not through the yarn strand. A blunt point ensures that you don't split the yarn.

Safety pins

Safety pins are handy for a variety of tasks. Pinned to your piece at strategic points, they can help you keep track of when to increase or decrease or signal the right side of reversible fabric. They work well as miniature stitch holders for small groups of stitches and for securing dropped stitches.

In knitting shops and specialty catalogs, you can find pins without coils in several sizes, which are less likely to catch on your yarn than regular safety pins.

Needle gauge and tension gauge

Needle gauges and tension gauges are indispensable. A *needle gauge* is a small rulerlike gadget with graduated holes in it for measuring the size of your knitting needles. If you knit a lot on circular needles, which frequently aren't labeled for size, or if you're prone to finding a lost double-pointed needle under the sofa cushions, a needle gauge is essential for size identification. Buy one that shows both metric and U.S. sizes.

A *tension gauge* (also called a *stitch gauge*) often comes as part of a needle gauge. It's a flat piece of metal or plastic with a 2-inch L-shaped window for measuring stitches and rows. You lay the tension gauge over your knitting, lining up the window along a row of stitches horizontally and vertically, and count the rows and stitches exposed. The drawback to using this tool is that 2 inches isn't always a large enough measure for an accurate gauge count. You can see a typical combination needle and tension gauge in Figure 2-5.

Cable needles

A *cable needle* is a short needle that's pointed at both ends, has a divot or curve toward the middle, and is used to hold stitches temporarily while you work on their neighbors. There are several different versions of the two main types: U-shaped and straight (see Figure 2-6). Try out a couple different styles to see which you like better.

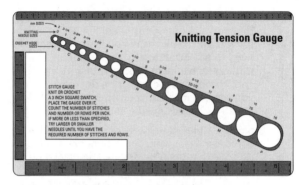

Figure 2-5: A common needle and tension gauge.

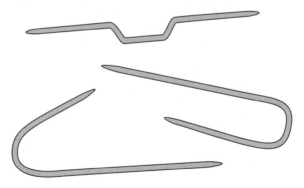

Figure 2-6: Cable needles.

Not necessary but nice to have

You can get by without buying the gadgets in this section, but you may find some of them worth the small investment. Figure 2-7 shows some of our favorite knitting gadgets:

- ✔ **Stitch markers:** A *stitch marker* is a small ring that you slip onto your needle between stitches to alert you to places in your knitting that you need to pay attention to: the beginning of a round, the beginning and end of a repeat, the spot to work an increase or a decrease. When you reach a marker, you slip it from the LH needle to the RH needle and carry on.

  Several styles of markers are on the market. Some are wafer thin, and others are small plastic coils that open up and can be placed on the needle in the middle of a row. Some are made from rubber and won't come whizzing off the end of your needle when you get to them.

- ✔ **Stitch holders:** *Stitch holders* resemble large safety pins but with a blunt point so as not to split the yarn and are used to secure stitches that you will work up or finish off later. They come in a variety of lengths, from 1¾ inches to 8 inches.

- ✔ **Point protectors:** *Point protectors* are small, rubber, pointed caps that fit over the tips of your needles to protect them and prevent your stitches from sliding off when you put down your work. They come in different sizes to fit your needles.

- ✔ **I-cord maker:** If you find yourself making lots of I-cords for bag handles or just for decoration, a hand-cranked I-cord maker will more than pay for itself in time saved. Available at many craft and yarn stores, these small machines make quick work of I-cord. For more information on I-cords and how to make them, head to Chapter 9.

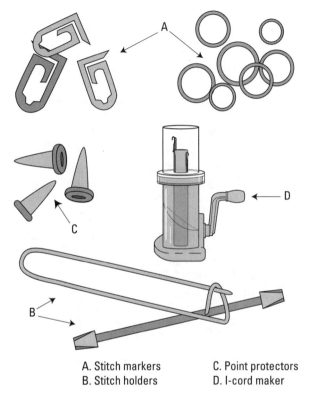

A. Stitch markers   C. Point protectors
B. Stitch holders   D. I-cord maker

Figure 2-7: Nonessential but handy knitting accessories.

Blocking Equipment

Blocking is the process of using steam or water to smooth out and gently uncurl and flatten your knitted pieces so that you can easily join them together. Blocking equipment makes the difference between a tiresome, awkward task and an easy, streamlined one. The basic blocking equipment includes the following:

- ✔ **Steam iron:** You probably already have a steam iron. The more steam the better.

- ✔ **Blocking board:** A blocking board is *not* your ironing board. It's a flat surface made from a material that you can stick a pin into. It should be large enough to hold at least one pinned-out sweater piece. Ideally, it should be marked with a 1-inch grid so that you can pin out your knitted piece to its proper dimensions without using your tape measure. If you have enough space, you can leave the blocking board up all the time for checking your project's measurements as you go along. Ready-made blocking boards or kits for making them are available. In a pinch, you can use your bed, but a real blocking board is better.

- ✔ **Blocking wires:** Blocking wires are long, slightly flexible stainless steel wires in various lengths. Threaded through the edges of your knitted piece, blocking wires allow you to pin the piece into shape so that the edges don't become scalloped at the pin sites. They're a wonderful invention and well worth the investment.

- ✔ **T-pins:** Large T-shaped straight pins help you pin out the edges of your project pieces. T-pins are easy to get a grip on, and because they don't have any plastic parts (like straight pins with colorful plastic heads), they won't melt under your iron while you're steaming your knitted piece.

Chapter 3

Taking the Mystery out of Patterns and Gauge

· ·

In This Chapter

▶ Making sense of knitting pattern lingo

▶ Reading written patterns

▶ Taking time to get the right gauge

· ·

*Y*ou can knit — and enjoy it — for years without ever cracking a knitting book or learning about gauge, but unless you have a mentor who can help you increase your repertoire and fine-tune your technique, you'll be limited as to what you can create. Simple scarves and plain afghans can inspire you for only so long. Eventually, you'll want to branch out and try new things, and you'll find your inspiration in the many knitting books and magazines that are out there.

But to re-create those things — the lacework shawls, the finely shaped garments, the argyle socks, or the cabled jackets — you need to know how to decode instructions and how to control the sizing of a knitted piece. Fortunately, this chapter is devoted entirely to those topics.

Reading Stitch Patterns

Directions for stitch patterns can be given in two different ways: written form and chart form. Written
instructions tell you what to do with the stitches in
each row as you come to them, whereas a chart
shows a picture of each stitch and how it's worked.
Some people prefer written instructions, and others
like to follow a graphed "picture" of the pattern. *Note:*
The patterns in this book are all written; if you want
to learn to read a charted pattern, check out the full-
size version of *Knitting For Dummies,* 2nd Edition
(Wiley).

Stitch patterns are based on *repeats* — both
stitch repeats and row repeats. A given stitch
sequence repeats horizontally across a row. A
series of rows of given stitch sequences
repeats vertically. Together they make up a
stitch pattern that determines what your knitted fabric will look like: smooth, bumpy,
cabled, or striped.

Deciphering Knitterese: Common abbreviations and shorthand

In order to save space, patterns are written in a con-
densed form with many abbreviations and a lot of
shorthand. As you work with patterns, you'll become
familiar with the most common abbreviations — for
example, RS (right side), WS (wrong side), beg (beginning), and rep (repeat). Pattern instructions explain
any unusual abbreviations or ones that may vary
from pattern to pattern. Table 3-1 presents some of
the most common pattern abbreviations.

Table 3-1   Common Knitting Abbreviations

Abbreviation	What It Means	Abbreviation	What It Means
beg	beginning	pwise	purlwise (as if to purl)
CC	contrasting color	rem	remain(s) or remaining
ch	chain	rep	repeat
cn	cable needle	RH	right-hand
dec	decrease(s), decreased, or decreasing	RS	right side(s)
dpns	double-pointed needles	rnd(s)	round(s)
foll	follows or following	sc	single crochet
inc	increase(s), increased, or increasing	sl	slip, slipped, or slipping
k	knit	sl st	slip stitch
k2tog	knit 2 stitches together	ssk	slip, slip, knit the slipped stitches together
k-b	knit in stitch below	St st	stockinette stitch
kwise	knitwise (as if to knit)	st(s)	stitch(es)
LH	left-hand	tbl	through the back of the loop

(continued)

Table 3-1 *(continued)*

Abbreviation	What It Means	Abbreviation	What It Means
lp(s)	loop(s)	tog	together
MC	main color	WS	wrong side(s)
m1 (or m)	make 1 stitch (increase 1 stitch)	wyib	with yarn in back
p	purl	wyif	with yarn in front
pat(s)	pattern(s)	yb	yarn back
p-b	purl in stitch below	yf	yarn forward
pm	place marker	yo	yarn over
psso	pass slipped stitch over (used for decreasing)		

In addition, knitting patterns use certain phrases that can be confusing until you've had some experience with them. Here are some of the more common phrases that you'll come across in knitting patterns and garments:

✔ **as established:** When your instructions set up a series of steps or patterns to work, rather than repeat them row by row, they tell you to continue working *as established.*

Example: If you're knitting a cardigan with the center front band knitted in, the stitches for the center front band may be worked in a different pattern from the rest of the sweater body. After the pattern tells you how many border stitches to work in the border pattern and how many stitches to work in the sweater body pattern, it tells you to continue to work the patterns in the front piece *as established.*

✔ **at same time:** This phrase indicates that two things need to happen at the same time. Be on the lookout for this phrase; it's easy to get going on one task and forget to pay attention to the other.

Example: "dec 1 st every other row 4 times, *at same time,* when piece measures same length as back to shoulder, work shoulder shaping as for back." Translation: The neckline shaping (dec 1 st) continues as the shoulder shaping begins.

✔ **back of your work:** The back of your work is the side of your work that faces away from you as you hold your needles. Don't confuse this with the right side (RS) and wrong side (WS) of your work, which refer to how the piece is worn or which side should be presented as the front.

✔ **bind off from each neck edge:** When you shape the neckline on a pullover, you work both edges of the neckline at the same time, but you shape the right side (as you wear it) on right-side rows and the left side on wrong-side rows. Although this instruction may sound tricky, it's quite obvious and simple when you're doing it. You may see it in a form like this: "bind off from each neck edge 3 sts once, 2 sts twice. . . ."

✔ **end with a WS row:** Finish the section you're working on by working a wrong-side row last. The next row you work should be a right-side row.

✔ **front of your work:** The front of your work is the side of your work that faces you as you hold your needles. It can be the wrong side or the right side.

✔ **inc (or dec) every 4 (6, 8, or whatever) rows:** This is how the increases (or decreases) along a sleeve seam are written. Increase or decrease on a (usually) right-side row, and then work 3 (5, 7, or whatever) rows without shaping.

✔ **inc (or dec) every other row:** Increase or decrease on the (usually) right-side row, and then work the following row without increasing or decreasing.

✔ **pat rep (pattern repeat):** When instructions tell you to repeat a certain stitch pattern, it's written this way. Pattern repeat refers to what's given between an asterisk and a semicolon (* . . . ;) in written patterns and between heavy black lines in a chart.

✔ **pick up and knit:** Use a separate strand of yarn to create a row of stitches on a needle by pulling loops through along a knitted edge, usually the front of a cardigan or a neckline.

✔ **pm (place marker):** A *marker* is a plastic ring or tied loop of yarn that sits between stitches on your needle to indicate the beginning of a round in circular knitting or to mark pattern repeats. When you see the instruction to place a marker, as in "join, pm, and begin round," you simply place a marker at that location. (As you knit, you slip the marker from one needle to the other. But usually your pattern doesn't tell you to do that — your common sense does.)

✔ **preparation row:** Some stitch patterns require a set-up row that's worked only at the beginning of the pattern and isn't part of the repeat.

✔ **reverse shaping:** When you knit a cardigan, you work two pieces that mirror each other. Most patterns have you work the side that carries the buttons before you work the side that carries the buttonholes. Instead of writing a separate set of instructions for each side, the pattern asks you to work the shaping in the opposite direction on the second piece, as in "work to correspond to front, reversing all shaping." This means that you work bind-offs and neck shaping on the reverse side of the fabric as well. If you work the shaping on the wrong side in one piece, you work it on the right side when you reverse the shaping.

✔ **right:** When a pattern specifies a right front, it means the front that would be on your right side *as you would wear the finished piece.* When in doubt, hold your knitting up to you (wrong side to your body) to determine whether it's the right or left front.

✔ **when armhole measures . . . :** This phrase signals that your instructions are about to change. Measure the armhole *not* from the beginning of the piece but from the marker you've (we hope) put near the middle of the row on which the armhole began. (The pattern should have told you to place this marker.)

✔ **work as for . . . :** This phrase usually refers to working the front piece the same as the back. It saves writing out the same instructions twice. You may see it in a form like this: "work as for back until piece measures 21½ inches from beg."

✔ **work even:** Continue in whatever stitch pattern you're using without doing any shaping.

✔ **work to end:** Work in whatever stitch pattern you're using to the end of the row.

You may run into other phrases that aren't as clear as they could be, but experience will make you familiar with them. Eventually, you'll be surprised at how well you understand this language, and you'll wonder why it ever seemed confusing.

Following written stitch patterns

Written instructions give you row-by-row directions
for a single repeat. They follow certain conventions
and use lots of abbreviations (see the preceding section). The key to understanding written instructions
is paying attention to commas, asterisks, and brackets or parentheses; they mean more than you may
think. Here's a punctuation translation:

- ✔ **Single steps are separated by commas.** The
  instruction "Sl 1 wyif, k5" tells you to slip a
  stitch with the yarn on the front side of the
  work, and *then* to knit 5 stitches as normal
  (meaning you have to move the yarn to the back
  before knitting, even though the instructions
  don't tell you to).

- ✔ **An asterisk (*) indicates that whatever follows gets repeated (rep).** For example, the
  instruction "K1, * sl 1, k3; rep from * to last st,
  k1" means that you knit 1 stitch, then you
  work the stitches between the asterisks (slip
  1 stitch and knit 3 stitches) over and over
  until you reach the last stitch of the row,
  which you knit.

- ✔ **Brackets (or parentheses) function much like
  the asterisks except that you're repeating a
  series of stitches a specified number of times.**
  For example, the instruction "* K5, (p1, k1)
  twice, p1; repeat from * to end of row" means
  that, after you knit 5, you purl 1/knit 1 *two
  times,* followed by another purl 1, and then
  you repeat this entire sequence across the
  entire row.

The following example shows a stitch pattern in written form:

Row 1 (RS): * K2, p2; rep from * to end of row.

Row 2 (WS): * P2, k2; rep from * to end of row.

Translation: On the first row (the right side is facing you on the first row in this pattern), you knit 2 stitches, purl 2 stitches, knit 2 stitches, purl 2 stitches, and so on to the end of the row. (Your row would have to be a multiple of 4 stitches for these instructions to come out evenly.) On the next row (wrong side facing now), you begin by purling 2 stitches, then knitting 2 stitches, purling 2 stitches, knitting 2 stitches, and so on to the end of the row.

 As you read patterns, pay attention to row designations. To save space, many written instructions combine rows that repeat the same stitches. For example, this ribbon eyelet pattern combines a couple of rows:

Cast on multiple of 2 sts, plus 2 sts.

Row 1: Knit.

Row 2: Purl.

Rows 3 and 4: Knit.

Row 5: P1, * yo, p2tog; repeat from * to last st, p1.

Row 6: K2, * k1 tbl, k1; repeat from * to end of row.

Row 7: Knit.

Row 8: Purl.

Rep Rows 1–8.

 As you can imagine, the more intricate the pattern, the more complicated the instructions. But if you read your instructions carefully, work each step between commas as a complete step, look at your work, and think about what you're doing, you won't have any problems.

Gauge: Getting the Size Right

Every knitted fabric is made up of stitches and rows. *Gauge* is the number of stitches and rows it takes to make 1 square inch of knitted fabric. Figure 3-1 shows the stitches and rows that make up 1 square inch of a stockinette swatch (a sample made specifically to test gauge). Stockinette and most other knitted fabrics have more vertical rows than stitches per inch. Understanding how to measure and work with gauge is what allows you to go from a knitted swatch or sample to a finished project that measures what you want it to.

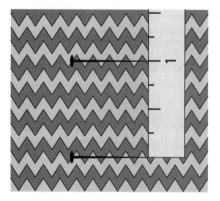

Figure 3-1: One square inch of stockinette measured.

If you've spent some time around knitters, you may already know that mention of the word *gauge* often elicits a groan. Gauge has a bad reputation among many knitters for three reasons. First, it represents an unpleasant *should.* Second, it's a tedious task that has to be accomplished before the fun part of the project — the *knitting* — can begin. Finally, it involves math.

However, getting comfortable with gauge gives you a leg up in knitting. Without knowing your gauge, you couldn't

- ✔ Knit away on your project comfortable in the knowledge that when you've worked the thousands of stitches required to complete it, it will fit.

- ✔ Substitute another yarn for the one given in the pattern.

- ✔ Use the size needle that makes the best fabric for your chosen yarn, even if it means you don't match the pattern's gauge.

The first step in any knitting project is to determine the gauge of the knitted fabric you're making. Gauge (sometimes called *tension*) is listed at the beginning of a pattern before the instructions begin. It's given as a number of stitches and rows over 4 square inches or 10 square centimeters, and it tells what needle and what stitch pattern were used to determine the gauge. Check your pattern to see how many stitches and rows should make up 4 inches of knitted fabric. You need to measure *your* gauge against that given in the directions.

 Gauge isn't always important, such as when you're making a scarf, an afghan, a bag, or anything else for which a precise size isn't essential. But when size *does* matter, the right or wrong gauge can make or break the finished piece.

Things that affect gauge

Gauge varies depending on the yarn, the needle size, and the stitch pattern you use.

✔ **Yarn:** Yarns of different weights produce different gauges. A bulkier yarn produces a larger stitch, for example, while a finer yarn produces a smaller stitch. Head to Chapter 2 for detailed information on yarn weights and the effect weight can have on the knitted fabric.

✔ **Needles and stitch size:** The same yarn knitted on different size needles will have different gauges. Because you make a knit stitch by wrapping yarn around a needle, the size (circumference) of the needle determines the size of the stitch.

Figure 3-2 shows how needle size can affect the way the finished fabric looks. The smaller the needle is, the tighter the stitches and the denser the knitted fabric. The larger the needle is, the looser the stitches and the drapier (and stretchier) the fabric.

Figure 3-2: Smaller needles result in tighter stitches; bigger needles in looser stitches.

✔ **Stitch patterns and stitch size:** The same yarn knitted on the same needles but in different stitch patterns will have different gauges. For example, cables and ribs pull in, requiring more stitches to make a square inch; lace and slip stitch or garter stitch patterns spread the fabric out, so they require fewer stitches to make an inch. Figure 3-3 compares the gauges of two different patterns that use the same number of stitches.

Figure 3-3: Gauge on different stitch patterns.

Gauge also can vary with the time of day you're knitting, how long you've been knitting at a stretch, and what you're thinking about. The tension you put on the yarn traveling around the needle contributes to stitch size, so being tired or tense can affect the flow of your yarn and stitch size.

Making a gauge swatch

To find out whether your gauge matches the pattern, you begin by making a gauge swatch. A gauge swatch is a small sample that you work using the same pattern, yarn, and needles you intend to use for your project.

It's important that you use the *same* yarn for your gauge swatch as for your project, not the same brand in a different color. Different dyes can affect how a specific yarn knits up, and believe it or not, a yarn in one color can give you a different gauge from the same yarn in a different color.

To make your swatch, follow these steps:

1. **Cast on the appropriate number of stitches.**

   In general, cast on the number of stitches given in the pattern for 4 inches, plus 6 more stitches. For example, if the gauge is given as 18 stitches and 22 rows over 4 inches, cast on 24 stitches.

   If the stitch pattern needs to be worked in a specific multiple, cast on any multiple that will yield a swatch larger than 4 inches in order to get an accurate gauge measurement. For example, if the pattern is worked on a multiple of 6 stitches plus 1 more, and the gauge given is 4 stitches to an inch, cast on *at least* 25 stitches (a multiple of 6 [+ 1]). At 4 stitches to the inch, your swatch will be more than 4 inches wide, giving you a good area for measuring.

2. **Work in the stitch pattern specified for the number of rows required to make 4 inches, plus 6 more rows.**

   For the same gauge specifications as in Step 1 (18 stitches and 22 rows over 4 inches), you work in the given pattern for 28 rows.

   These extra stitches and rows will give you a border around the area you're measuring. Edge stitches are frequently distorted and shouldn't be included in what you measure for gauge unless your swatch is a good 6 inches square.

3. **Bind off loosely or cut the strand of yarn, leaving an 8-inch tail, and draw it through the loops of the last row.**

4. **Block the swatch in the same manner you plan to use for your finished project.**

   Your stitches may shrink a bit when they're steamed. *Now* you're ready to measure it.

 Many patterns often give dimensions in centimeters rather than inches, or include metric measurements alongside U.S. ones. You can calculate inches from centimeters by dividing the centimeter number by 2.5. For example, 10 centimeters divided by 2.5 equals 4 inches. Or just use a ruler with centimeters.

Measuring your gauge

To measure your swatch, smooth it out on a flat surface (your lap is not flat); a blocking or ironing board is good for this task. Pin the edges down if they're curling in — be careful not to stretch your swatch — and follow these steps:

1. **Lay a ruler along a row of stitches and mark the beginning and end of 4 inches with pins.**

   If your second pin lands at half a stitch, don't be tempted to stretch or slightly squish your knitting to make the 4 inches end on a whole stitch.

2. **Note the number of stitches in 4 inches, fractions and all.**

3. **Lay your ruler along a vertical line of stitches, aligning the bottom of the ruler with the bottom of a stitch (the bottom of a V), and put a pin in**

to show where the first stitch begins. Place
another pin 4 inches up.

4. **Count the stitches between the pins and note
the number of rows.**

These steps give you gauge over a 4-inch (10-centimeter)
square. Check to see whether your 4-inch gauge
matches the one in the pattern. If it does, thank your
lucky stars. If it doesn't, head to the next section.

Matching your pattern's gauge

If your gauge swatch doesn't match the one specified
in the pattern you want to use and you want your
project to come out the same size as the pattern measures, you must change the needle size you're working on and make another swatch. If your first swatch
is smaller than specified, use larger needles. If your
swatch is larger than specified, use smaller needles.

Keep adjusting your needle size and remaking your
swatch until you get the number of stitches and rows
in a 4-inch square that your pattern requires. If you
can't get both stitch and row gauge to match the pattern's gauge, work with the needle that gives you the
right *stitch* gauge.

The cumulative effect of knitting at a gauge as
small as half a stitch less than the pattern calls for
can be disastrous. For example, if your project
piece is supposed to measure 20 inches and calls
for a gauge of 5 stitches per inch, your finished
piece will measure 22 inches if you're knitting at
4 stitches per inch. And if you're off by 2 inches
on both the front and back of a sweater, the total
difference between the pattern and your sweater
will be 4 inches overall. That's why gauge gets so
much attention in knitting books and why taking
the time to measure it is so important.

Measuring gauge on highly textured yarns

With fuzzy or highly textured yarns, it can be difficult to see your stitches clearly enough to take an accurate measurement by counting stitches. In this case, the following steps enable you to measure your gauge:

1. **Make a swatch larger than 4 inches and write down the total number of stitches and rows in your swatch.**

2. **Measure the entire swatch side to side and top to bottom.**

3. **Use a calculator to plug your numbers into the formulas that follow:**

   To find *stitch gauge* (number of horizontal stitches per inch): Divide the number of stitches in the swatch by the width of the swatch in inches. This gives you the number of stitches per inch.

   To find *row gauge* (number of vertical stitches per inch): Divide the number of rows by the overall length of the swatch in inches. This gives you the number of rows per inch.

To find your gauge over 4 inches, multiply stitches per inch or rows per inch by 4.

Designing with gauge in mind

As you begin to knit projects, you may find yourself imagining sweaters and hats you'd like to make but can't find a pattern for. Making your own pattern for a project isn't all that difficult. No matter how fancy the pattern stitch or shaping, how large or small the project, it all comes down to stitches and inches. Figure out your gauge on the yarn and needles you want to use, and then determine the dimensions of the finished project.

To determine the number of stitches to cast on for a project you're imagining, work the formula for determining gauge in reverse. Decide how wide you want your piece to be, and then multiply that number by your gauge. For example, if you're imagining a scarf in one of the basic stitch patterns in Chapter 5, make a gauge swatch. If your gauge is 5 stitches to the inch and you want your scarf to be 7 inches wide, cast on 35 stitches and start knitting.

Chapter 4

The Fundamentals: Casting On, Knitting, Purling, and Binding Off

. . . .

In This Chapter

▶ Casting stitches on and off your needles

▶ Getting the hang of basic knitting techniques

▶ Changing things up with basic purling techniques

. . . .

So here you are, a ball of yarn in one hand and two knitting needles in the other. To be a successful knitter, the first things you need to do are figure out how to get the one (yarn) onto the other (the needles) and, after achieving that, how to make the thing grow. The answers? Casting on and knitting and purling. Knit and purl stitches are the two stitches upon which all other knitting techniques are based. When you're comfortable with these stitches, you can create any number of amazing things.

Knitting is hugely relaxing — after you know the basics. As you pick up the techniques and practice them, keep these things in mind:

✔ Learning to knit can be a little stressful. Your fingers have to work in ways they're not accustomed to, and the illustrations that are decluttered for clarity make actual yarn-on-needles resemble a tangled mess — even if nothing's wrong. When you feel yourself getting tense or frustrated, set your knitting aside and do something else for a while.

✔ Throughout this chapter and the rest of the book, the abbreviation LH refers to the left hand, and RH refers to the right hand. We use these abbreviations when talking about the needles. You can find a list of other common abbreviations in Chapter 3.

Casting On

Creating the first row of stitches is called *casting on.* There are various ways to cast on, and different knitters have their favorites. In this section, we introduce you to a cast-on method that's great for beginners and works for just about any project you'll make.

Here are a couple tips about casting on:

✔ **Cast on your stitches evenly.** They make up the bottom edge of your knitting, and neatness counts.

✔ **Don't cast on too tightly.** Doing so makes the first row hard to work because you have to force your needle tip through the loop. If you find yourself doing this, you may want to start over and cast on with a needle one size larger to counteract the tension. Then switch to the requested size for the actual knitting.

✔ **When you're casting on a lot of stitches, place a stitch marker at particular intervals — like every 50 stitches.** That way, if you get interrupted or distracted as you're counting (and you will, sometimes multiple times), you don't have to begin counting again at the first stitch. As you work the first row, just drop the markers off the needle.

The two-strand cast-on method (sometimes called the *long-tail* method) is a great all-around cast-on for your starting repertoire. It's elastic, attractive, and easy to knit from. For this cast-on method, you need only one needle: the RH needle.

To cast on using the two-strand method, follow these steps:

1. **Measure off enough yarn for the bottom part of your piece and make a slip knot on your needle.**

   To figure how long the "tail" should be, you need approximately 1 inch for every stitch you cast on plus a little extra. Alternatively, you can measure the bottom of the knitted piece and multiply this by 4.

   To make the slip knot, make a pretzel-shaped loop and place your needle into the loop, as shown in Figure 4-1a. Then gently pull on both ends of the yarn until the stitch is firmly on the needle but still slides easily back and forth, as shown in Figure 4-1b.

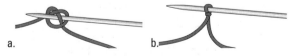

a.   b.

Figure 4-1: Get the slip knot (the first stitch) on your needle.

2. Holding the needle in your right hand with the tip pointing away from your hand, insert your left hand's thumb and index finger into the "tent" formed by the two yarn ends falling from the slip knot on your needle.

3. With your left hand's ring and pinkie fingers, catch the yarn ends and hold them to your palm so they don't flap around underneath (see Figure 4-2a).

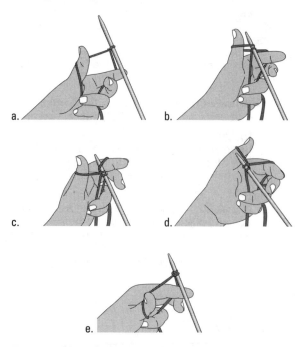

Figure 4-2: "Catch" a loop from your left hand.

4. **With your right hand, pull the needle between your left thumb and index finger so that the "tent" sides aren't droopy.**

5. **With the RH needle tip, go around the yarn on your thumb from the left (see Figure 4-2b), then around the yarn on your index finger from the right (see Figure 4-2c), and pull the new loop through (see Figure 4-2d).**

   Figure 4-2e shows the finished stitch.

6. **Tighten this new loop (your first cast-on stitch) onto the needle — but not too tight!**

   You'll quickly find that if you don't let go of the yarn after creating the stitch, you can use your thumb to tighten the stitch onto your needle.

   Although this is the first cast-on stitch, it's the second stitch on the RH needle because you also have the initial slip knot.

7. **Repeat Steps 5 and 6 until you have the number of stitches you need (see Figure 4-3).**

   If you need to put your work down, or if you lose your place, you may have to pull the stitches off the needle and start from Step 2 instead.

   Although casting on may feel awkward at first and you have to pay attention to each movement, with time and practice, you'll no longer have to think about what your hands are doing. You'll be surprised at how quickly you'll learn the movements and make them smoothly and effortlessly while you think about something entirely unknitterish.

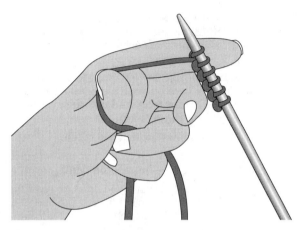

Figure 4-3: Finished cast-on stitches.

Now You're Knitting and Purling

Knitted (and purled) stitches are made by using a continuous strand of yarn and two needles to pull new loops through old loops. That's it. The following sections explain how to create both stitches.

Here are a couple of tips to keep in mind as you learn how to knit:

✔ **Finish working an entire row before putting down your knitting.** It's too easy to stop midway and pick up your knitting later to find you can't tell the LH from the RH needle. Here's an easy way to tell: The yarn is always hanging down from the last stitch you made, no matter what kind of stitch it is. So if you've finished the entire row as we recommend, when you pick up your needles again, the needle with stitches will be in your left hand.

✔ **Practice until the movements feel comfortable and relaxed.** When you feel like you're getting the hang of it, try an experiment. Close your eyes or look at the ceiling while you knit — let your fingers feel their way. Can you knit without looking yet? Eventually you'll be able to. If you make this your goal, you can get lots of knitting done during movies!

Knitting know-how

To knit, with the yarn in your right hand, hold the needle with the cast-on stitches in your left hand, pointing to the right. Make sure that the first stitch is no more than 1 inch from the tip of the needle. Then follow these steps:

1. **Insert the tip of the empty (RH) needle into the first stitch on the LH needle from left to right and front to back, forming a T with the tips of the needles.**

   The RH needle will be behind the LH needle (see Figure 4-4).

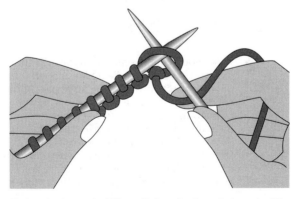

Figure 4-4: Insert the RH needle into the first stitch on the LH needle.

2. **With your right hand, bring the yarn to the front from the *left side* of the RH needle, and then over the RH needle to the right and down between the needles.**

   You can try to maneuver the yarn with your right forefinger, as shown in Figure 4-5a, or just hold it between your thumb and forefinger for now.

3. **Keeping a slight tension on the wrapped yarn, bring the tip of the RH needle with its wrap of yarn through the loop on the LH needle to the front.**

   The RH needle is now in front of the LH needle (see Figure 4-5b). Keep the tip of the left forefinger on the point of the RH needle to help guide the needle through the old stitch and prevent losing the wrap of yarn.

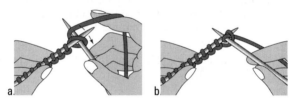

Figure 4-5: Complete a knit stitch.

 When you bring the new loop through the old, bring the RH needle up far enough that the new stitch forms on the large part of the needle, not just on the tip. If you work too close to the tips, your new stitches form on the narrowest part of your needles, making them too tight to knit with ease. Tight stitches have brought many a new knitter to a frustrated halt. By the same token, don't knit too far from the tips. Keep the stitches on the LH needle close enough to the tip so that you don't struggle and stretch to pull off the old stitch.

Note that when you've finished making a knit stitch, the yarn is coming out the *back* on the side of the needle facing away from you. Be sure that the yarn hasn't ended up in front of your work or over the needle before you start your next stitch.

4. **Slide the RH needle to the right until the old loop on the LH needle drops off.**

   You now have a new stitch/loop on the RH needle — the old stitch hangs below it (see Figure 4-6). Congratulations! You've just made your first knitted stitch!

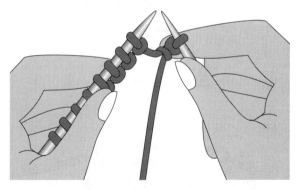

Figure 4-6: Your first knitted stitch!

5. **Repeat Steps 1 through 4 until you've knitted all the stitches from your LH needle.**

   Your LH needle is now empty, and your RH needle is full of beautiful, new stitches.

6. **Turn your work (that is, switch hands so that the needle with stitches is in your left hand) and knit the new row.**

   When you turn your work, the yarn strand coming out of the first stitch to knit is hanging down in the front (see Figure 4-7). Also notice that the stitch just below the first stitch (labeled "Big loop" in Figure 4-7) on your LH needle is larger than the rest and can obscure your view of where your needle should go.

   You may be tempted to pull the yarn strand over the needle to the back to tighten up the stitch. If you do this, it will look like you have 2 stitches on your needle instead of 1. Keep the strand in front and gently pull down on it, and the big loop if necessary, to better see the opening of the first stitch. Be sure to insert the point of the RH needle in the loop on the LH needle and not into the stitch below.

Stitch

Big loop

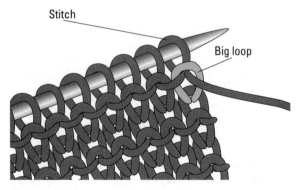

Figure 4-7: The first stitch of the next row.

7. **Repeat these steps for several more rows (or all afternoon) until you're comfortable with the movements.**

   Aim to make these steps one continuous movement, to make even stitches, and to stay relaxed! After you've knitted a few rows, take a look at what you've created: It's the *garter stitch,* and it's one of the most common — and easiest — stitch patterns. You can find it and other common stitch patterns in Chapter 5.

If you're having trouble getting into the knitting "flow," change the way you carry the yarn in your hand. Or prop the knob of your RH needle under your armpit or on your hipbone to keep it stationary while you use the left hand to initiate the movements. Study how other knitters do things, and be willing to try it different ways until you find your knitting "home." When you understand how the yarn travels around your needle to make new loops, you'll sort out the best way to hold your yarn and needles for comfort, speed, and even stitches.

Perfect purling

Purling is working a knit stitch backwards: Instead of going into the stitch from front to back, you enter it from back to front. Combining knit stitches with purl stitches enables you to make a wide variety of textured stitch patterns, many of the most common of which we include in Chapter 5.

To purl, follow these steps:

1. **Hold the needle with the cast-on or existing stitches in your left hand, pointing to the right. Insert the tip of the RH needle into the first loop**

on the LH needle from right to left and back to front, forming a T with the needle tips.

The RH needle is in front of the LH needle, and the working yarn is in front of your needles (see Figure 4-8a). This is the reverse of what you do when you form a knit stitch.

2. **With your right hand, wrap the yarn around the back of the RH needle from right to left and down (see Figure 4-8b).**

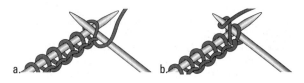

Figure 4-8: Purling.

3. **Keeping a slight tension on the wrap of yarn, bring the tip of the RH needle with its wrap of yarn down and through the loop on the LH needle to the *back* side of the LH needle (see Figure 4-9a).**

4. **Slide the old loop off the tip of the LH needle.**

A new stitch is made on the RH needle. You can see how it should look in Figure 4-9b.

Figure 4-9: Finishing your purl stitch.

5. **Repeat Steps 1 through 4 until you're comfortable with the movements.**

 When you purl, the yarn strand comes out of the
new stitches on the side of the knitting facing
you. When you knit, the yarn comes out of the
new stitches on the side facing away from you.

A purled swatch looks just like a knitted swatch.
Why? Because purling is simply the reverse of knitting. Whether you knit all the rows or purl all the
rows, you're working a garter stitch (see Chapter 5 for
more on the garter stitch).

Joining yarn

Balls of yarn are finite. When you're knitting away and you
least expect it, you'll run out of yarn. Time to start the next
ball of yarn in a process called *joining yarn*. When possible,
start a new ball of yarn on an edge that will be enclosed in a
seam, but try *not* to start a new ball of yarn on an edge that
will be exposed.

To join yarn at an edge, knit the first stitch of the next row
with both ends held together, drop the old strand, and carry
on. Or knit the first few stitches with the new yarn only, stop,
and tie the two ends together temporarily in a bow to secure
them. Either way, leave the ends at least 4 or 5 inches long
so that you can weave them in later.

If you run out of yarn in the middle of a row, your options are
the same: Tie a temporary knot with both yarns, leaving 4- or
5-inch ends; or knit the next stitch with both strands, drop
the old one, and continue knitting from the new ball.

Binding (or Casting) Off

To finish your knitted piece, you have to *bind off*, which is securing the stitches in the last row worked so that they don't unravel. It's easy to do if you follow these basic steps:

1. **Knit the first 2 stitches from the LH needle. These become the first 2 stitches on your RH needle (see Figure 4-10a).**

2. **With your LH needle in front of your RH needle, insert the LH needle into the first stitch worked on the RH needle (the one on the right, as shown in Figure 4-10b).**

3. **Bring this loop over the second stitch and off the tip of the RH needle, as shown in Figure 4-10c.**

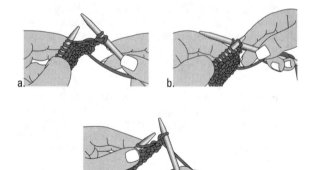

Figure 4-10: Bind off a stitch.

At this point, you have 1 stitch bound off and 1 stitch remaining on your RH needle.

4. **Knit the next stitch on the LH needle so that you again have 2 stitches on your RH needle.**

5. **Repeat Steps 2 through 4 until you have 1 stitch remaining on your RH needle.**

6. **Cut the yarn a few inches from the needle and pull the tail through the last stitch to lock it.**

 If the piece you've just bound off is to be sewn to another piece, leave a tail that's 12 inches long or longer for a built-in strand to sew up a seam.

 Just as a casting on evenly gives the bottom edge of your piece a neat appearance, binding off evenly ensures a neat top edge. Here are some suggestions for getting an attractive edge:

✔ **Tighten up the loop below the last bind-off stitch.** This loop is often (for some mysterious reason) big and baggy, so when you come to the last stitch (1 stitch on the RH needle and 1 stitch on the LH needle), slip the last stitch on the RH needle back to the LH needle. Insert the tip of the RH needle into the left stitch on the LH needle and bring it over the right stitch and off the needle — binding off in the reverse direction. Cut the yarn and draw the tail through the remaining loop.

✔ **Unless otherwise told to do so, always bind off according to the stitch pattern given.** If you would normally be working a purl row, purl the stitches as you bind off instead of knitting them.

✔ **Don't bind off too tightly (which, unfortunately, is easy to do).** Knitting should be elastic, especially around neck edges if you want to be able to get a sweater on and off comfortably (and who doesn't want that?). To avoid a tight and inelastic bound edge, try working the bind-off row on a needle one or more sizes larger than what you've been using.

Chapter 5

Basic Stitches You'll Use Again and Again

- -

In This Chapter

▶ Practicing common stitch patterns

▶ Using popular rib stitches to add interest and stretch

- -

*W*hen you know how to knit and purl (refer to Chapter 4), you can combine these stitches in a seemingly endless variety of textured stitch patterns. The stitch patterns in this chapter make a good starting repertoire.

The best way to understand how knit-and-purl patterns work is to knit them up yourself. Using a medium-weight, solid-color yarn, cast on a multiple of the stitches required for the pattern (but no less than 24) and knit up about 4 inches in the pattern. You can save your swatches in a knitting notebook for later reference, or you can sew them together to create a patchwork scarf or afghan.

Stitches Every Knitter Should Know: Garter, Stockinette, and Seed Stitches

Knitting and purling, which we cover in Chapter 4, open the door to all sorts of patterns that just involve alternating between knit and purl stitches. But as a beginning knitter, you only really need to know two: the *garter stitch,* which you create simply by knitting (or purling) every row, and the *stockinette stitch,* which you create by alternating a knit row with a purl row. Another stitch all knitters should have in their repertoire is the *seed stitch.* Although a little more complicated than the garter and stockinette stitches, it creates an interesting texture and is included in many patterns.

When knitting a stitch, the loose tail of yarn is in *back* of your work. When purling a stitch, the yarn is in *front* of your work. As you switch back and forth within a row, you need to move your yarn to the front or to the back as appropriate. Unfortunately for novice knitters who often forget to move the yarn accordingly, instructions don't explicitly tell you to bring your yarn to the front or back of your work. They assume that you know where the yarn should be when you're about to knit or purl a stitch. As you practice the patterns that combine both knit and purl stitches, make sure your yarn is in the proper position for each stitch before you start it, and refer to Chapter 4 for a quick review if necessary.

Garter stitch

Garter stitch is the most basic of all knitted fabrics. It's made by knitting every row. (You can create garter stitch by purling every row, too. Neat, huh?) You can recognize garter stitch by the horizontal ridges formed by the tops of the knitted loops on every other row (see Figure 5-1).

Figure 5-1: Garter stitch.

Garter stitch has a lot going for it in addition to being easy to create. It's reversible, lies flat, and has a pleasant rustic look. Unlike most knitted fabrics, garter stitch has a square gauge, meaning that there are usually twice as many rows as stitches in 1 inch. To count rows in garter stitch, count the ridges and multiply by 2, or count the ridges by twos. Refer to Chapter 3 for more about checking gauge.

Stockinette stitch

When you alternate a knit row with a purl row (knit the first row, purl the second, knit the third, purl the

fourth, and so on), you create *stockinette stitch* (abbreviated St st); see Figure 5-2. You see stockinette stitch
everywhere: in scarves, socks, sweaters, blankets,
hats — you name it. In fact, most beginning and inter-
mediate designs incorporate stockinette stitch.

Figure 5-2: Stockinette stitch.

Stockinette fabric looks and behaves in a particular
way; to successfully incorporate this stitch into your
knitting repertoire, pay attention to the following:

> ✔ **Stockinette stitch has a right and a wrong side**
> (though, of course, either side may be the
> "right" side depending on the intended design).
> The right side is typically the smooth side,
> called *stockinette* or *knit.* On this side, the
> stitches look like small Vs (see Figure 5-3). The
> bumpy side of stockinette stitch fabric, shown
> in Figure 5-4, is called *reverse stockinette* or *purl.*

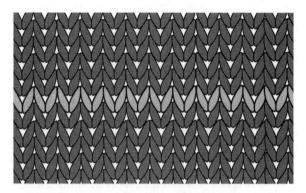

Figure 5-3: Stockinette stitch showing the knit (or smooth) side.

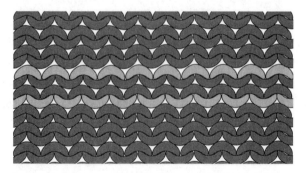

Figure 5-4: Reverse stockinette showing the purl (or bumpy) side.

 If you're working in stockinette stitch and you lose track of whether you knit the last row or purled it, not to worry. You can tell what to do next by looking at your knitting. Hold your needles in the ready-to-knit position (with the LH needle holding the stitches to be worked) and look at what's facing you. If you're looking at the knit (smooth) side, you knit. If you're looking at the purl (bumpy) side, you purl.

✔ **Stockinette fabric curls on the edges.** The top and bottom (horizontal) edges curl toward the front or smooth side. The side (vertical) edges roll toward the bumpy side. Sweater designers frequently use this rolling feature deliberately to create rolled hems or cuffs, and you can create easy cords or straps simply by knitting a very narrow (say, 4 or 6 stitches across) band in stockinette stitch.

But when you want the piece to lie flat, you need to counteract this tendency by working the 3 or 4 stitches on the edge in some stitch that lies flat (like garter stitch, discussed in the preceding section, or seed stitch, discussed in the next section).

To figure out the gauge of a swatch knitted in stockinette stitch, count the bumps from the wrong side. They're easier to see than the Vs on the smooth side.

Seed stitch

Seed stitch, shown in Figure 5-5, consists of single knits and purls alternating horizontally and vertically. Its name refers to the way the knitted fabric looks: The little purl bumps look like scattered seeds. Like garter stitch, seed stitch lies flat, making it a good edging for a sweater border and cuffs. It also looks the same from both sides, making it a nice choice for scarves and other pieces of which both sides are visible.

Figure 5-5: Seed stitch.

To create seed stitch:

Cast on an even number of sts.

Row 1: * K1, p1; rep from * to end of row.

Row 2: * P1, k1; rep from * to end of row.

Rep Rows 1 and 2 for pattern.

When working seed stitch, you alternate between knit and purl stitches in each row. The trick to creating the little "seeds" is to knit in the purl stitches of the previous row and purl in the knit stitches of the previous row.

Ribbed Stitches

Knit ribs are textured vertical stripes. Ribbing is made by alternating columns of knit stitches with columns of purl stitches. Instead of alternating knit rows with purl rows, as you do when you make horizontal stripes, when you make a ribbed pattern, you change from knit stitches to purl stitches *within* a row.

Ribbing is the edging par excellence on most sweaters because of its elasticity; it stretches to let you in and out of cuffs and neckbands and then springs back into place to hug you. It's also used for the body of many pieces, like sweaters, scarves, and hats.

The most common ribbing combinations are those that are even (that is, the rib uses the same number of knitted versus purl columns). Examples include 1 x 1 ribbing, in which single knit stitches alternate with single purl stitches, creating very narrow columns; and 2 x 2 ribbing, which alternates 2 knit stitches with 2 purl stitches. Although even columns are among the most common ribbed patterns, the columns don't have to be even. Many attractive and functional ribs have wider knit columns than purl columns.

The elasticity of the final ribbed fabric is affected by

- ✔ **Column width:** The narrower the column of stitches, the more elastic the ribbing.

- ✔ **Needle size:** Bigger needles result in less elasticity. Also, because ribbed edgings are intended to "hug" the body, you generally work them on needles one or two sizes smaller than the ones used for the body of the project.

The following sections explain how to create the most common ribbing patterns.

1 x 1 ribbing

The 1 x 1 rib pattern alternates single knit stitches with single purl stitches to create narrow ribs. Figure 5-6 shows this ribbing stretched out a bit so that you can see the purl rows (the horizontal lines in the background). When it isn't stretched out, the knit columns contract, hiding the purl columns.

Figure 5-6: 1 x 1 ribbing.

To create 1 x 1 ribbing:

Cast on an even number of sts.

Work every row: * K1, p1; rep from * to end of row.

Rep this row for the length of your piece.

After the first row, you can tell by looking at your knitting whether you should be making a knit stitch or a purl stitch. If the next stitch on your LH needle is a purl (bump) stitch, purl it. If it's a knit stitch, knit it.

2 x 2 ribbing

As you can see in Figure 5-7, 2 x 2 ribbing alternates 2 knit stitches with 2 purl stitches. It pulls in slightly less than 1 x 1 ribbing.

Figure 5-7: 2 x 2 ribbing.

To create 2 x 2 ribbing:

Cast on a multiple of 4 sts.

Work every row: * K2, p2; rep from * to end of row.

Rep this row for the length of your piece.

Note: If you want your piece to begin and end on 2 knit stitches, add 2 to the multiple that you cast on at the beginning.

4 x 2 and 2 x 4 ribbing

There's no reason to keep knit ribs and purl ribs the same number of stitches. You can work ribs in uneven combinations, such as 4 x 2, 2 x 4, and so on. Figure 5-8 shows a 4 x 2 ribbing.

Figure 5-8: 4 x 2 ribbing.

To create 4 x 2 ribbing:

Cast on a multiple of 6 sts, plus 4 sts. (You can work this pattern over a multiple of 6 stitches, but it won't be symmetrical.)

Row 1: * K4, p2; rep from * to last 4 sts, k4.

Row 2: * P4, k2; rep from * to last 4 sts, p4.

Rep Rows 1 and 2 for pattern.

If you turn this swatch over, you'll have a very different looking pattern — thin vertical stripes instead of thick ones.

4 x 4 ribbing

The 4 x 4 rib shown in Figure 5-9 gives you a vertical stripe pattern that pulls in very little. It's symmetrical in that it's a simple alternation of 4 knit stitches with 4 purl stitches.

Figure 5-9: 4 x 4 ribbing.

To create 4 x 4 ribbing:

> Cast on a multiple of 4 sts, plus 4 sts.
>
> **Row 1:** * K4, p4; rep from * to last 4 sts, k4.
>
> **Row 2:** * P4, k4; rep from * to last 4 sts, end p4.
>
> Rep Rows 1 and 2 for pattern.

Chapter 6

Techniques Every Knitter Should Know

*P*laying around with knit and purl patterns introduced in Chapter 5 can keep you busy for a long time, but you can do a lot more with knitted stitches. As you begin to explore different stitch patterns and follow patterns for projects and garments, you'll want to familiarize yourself with the different stitch maneuvers that crop up in instructions for more demanding knitted fabrics.

For projects that give you the opportunity to practice the maneuvers that we cover in this chapter, head to Chapter 9.

Slipping Stitches

If your directions tell you to *slip a stitch* (abbreviated sl st), they mean for you to move a stitch from the left-hand (LH) needle to the right-hand (RH) needle without knitting or purling it *and* without changing its orientation (that is, without twisting it).

To slip a stitch, insert the RH needle *purlwise* (as if you were going to purl) into the first stitch on the LH needle and slip it off the LH needle onto the RH needle. Unless your instructions specifically tell you to slip a stitch *knitwise,* always slip a stitch as if you were going to purl it. Figure 6-1 shows stitches being slipped both purlwise and knitwise.

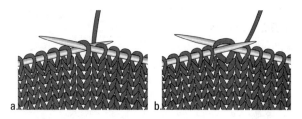

Figure 6-1: Slipping stitches purlwise (a) and knitwise (b).

Working Increases

Not all knitted pieces are square. Being able to increase (abbreviated inc) or decrease (abbreviated dec) stitches along the edge or within the body of a knitted piece enables you to create knitted pieces with edges that taper and expand. When you increase stitches, you add them to your needle. When you decrease stitches, you get rid of stitches on your needle.

The following sections outline the ways to work increases into your work. So, how do you know which one to use? If the increase is part of a fabric stitch pattern, the pattern will almost always tell you how to make the increase.

Bar increase

So-called because it leaves a telltale horizontal bar under the increased stitch, the *bar increase* is best for increases worked at the edge of your knitting, where it will be enclosed in a seam. Knitting directions for the bar increase read, "Knit 1 into the front and back of the stitch" or "k1fb."

To make a bar increase when you're working on the *knit* side, follow these steps:

1. **Knit 1 stitch as you normally would, but don't slide the old stitch off the LH needle.**

2. **Bring the tip of the RH needle behind the LH needle and enter the back of the stitch from right to left.**

   The front of the stitch is the part of the loop on *your* side of the needle. The back of the stitch is, well, on the side of the needle facing away from you.

3. **Knit the stitch as normal and slide it off the LH needle.**

   You've worked 2 stitches from a single stitch.

To make a bar increase when you're working on the *purl* side, follow these steps:

1. **Purl 1 stitch as you normally would, but don't slide the old stitch off the LH needle.**

2. **Keeping the RH needle behind the LH one, insert the tip of the RH needle through the back of the loop, entering it from left to right.**

3. **Purl that stitch again and slide it off the LH needle.**

   You've worked 2 stitches from a single stitch.

Working a make 1

To work the *make 1* increase (abbreviated m1), you create a new, separate stitch between 2 stitches that are already on the needle. When you get to the point where you want to make an increase, pull the LH and RH needles slightly apart. You'll notice a horizontal strand of yarn, called the *running thread,* connecting the first stitch on each needle. You use the running thread to make the new stitch. The increased stitch will be a twisted stitch that crosses to the right or to the left and leaves no little hole.

Twisting to the right

When you're working on the knit side and want your make 1 increase to twist to the right, work to the point between 2 stitches where you want to increase, and then follow these steps:

1. **Bring the tip of the LH needle under the running thread from back to front.**

   The running thread will be draped over the LH needle as if it were a stitch (see Figure 6-2a).

2. **Insert the RH needle through the draped strand from left to right (see Figure 6-2b) and knit as normal.**

Figure 6-2: Knitting a m1 increase that twists to the right.

If you want to work a right-twisting make 1 increase on the *purl* side, follow the preceding steps, except change Step 2 by purling the strand by going into the front loop (the part that's closest to you) from right to left and purling as normal (see Figure 6-3).

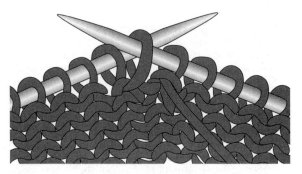

Figure 6-3: Purling a m1 increase that twists to the right.

Twisting to the left

If you're working on the knit side and want your make 1 increase to twist to the left, work to the point between 2 stitches where you want to increase, and then follow these steps:

1. **Insert the tip of the LH needle under the running thread from front to back (see Figure 6-4a).**

2. **With the RH needle, knit the strand through the back (see Figure 6-4b).**

Figure 6-4: Knitting a m1 increase that twists to the left.

Follow the same steps when you want your make 1 increase to twist to the left from the *purl* side, except change Step 2 by inserting the RH needle through the back loop from left to right and purling as normal.

Doing Decreases

A decrease is a method for getting rid of a stitch on your needle. You use decreases for shaping at the edges and/or in the middle of a knitted piece. They're also used in conjunction with increases in various stitch patterns, most notably in lace.

A decreased stitch looks like 1 stitch overlapping another. Depending on the design you're working with, you can make your decreases slant to the left or right. When a stitch overlaps to the right, the decrease slants to the right. When a stitch overlaps to the left, the decrease slants to the left.

Knitting 2 stitches together

When you knit 2 stitches together (abbreviated k2tog), they become 1 stitch. The stitch on the left overlaps the one on the right, and the decrease slants to the right. If you're working decreases in pairs (on either side of a neckline you're shaping, for example), use the k2tog on one side and the ssk decrease (see the later section, "Slip, slip, knit") on the other side.

To knit 2 stitches together on the right (knit) side of your knitted fabric, follow these steps:

1. **Insert the RH needle knitwise into the first 2 stitches on the LH needle at the same time.**

2. **Knit them together as if they were 1 stitch (see Figure 6-5).**

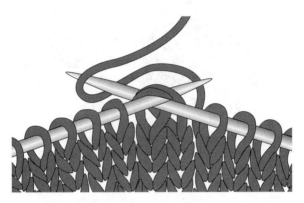

Figure 6-5: Knitting 2 stitches together (k2tog).

Purling 2 stitches together

Although most knitting patterns have you decrease on right-side rows only, sometimes you may be asked to work a decrease from the purl side. When you do, you can purl 2 stitches together (abbreviated p2tog) instead of knitting them together. When you look at a p2tog decrease from the knit side, the stitches slant to the right, just as they do with a k2tog decrease.

When you need to work a single p2tog decrease on the wrong (purl) side of your knitting, follow these steps:

1. **Insert the RH needle purlwise into the next 2 stitches on the LH needle (see Figure 6-6a).**

2. **Purl the 2 stitches together as if they were 1 stitch (see Figures 6-6b and 6-6c).**

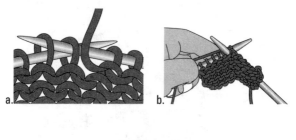

Figure 6-6: Purling 2 stitches together (p2tog).

Slip, slip, knit

Slip, slip, knit (abbreviated ssk) results in a left-slanting decrease. The ssk decrease is the mirror image of k2tog: It slants to the left. Use it when you want to work symmetrical decreases.

To work a ssk on the knit side, follow these steps:

1. **Slip the first stitch on the LH needle (as if to knit) to the RH needle without actually knitting it.**

2. **Do the same with the next stitch.**

   The 2 slipped stitches should look like the stitches in Figure 6-7a.

3. **Insert the LH needle into the front loops of these stitches (left to right), as in Figure 6-7b.**

4. **Wrap the yarn in the usual way around the RH needle and knit the 2 slipped stitches together.**

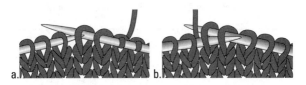

Figure 6-7: Working a slip, slip, knit (ssk) decrease.

To work an ssk on the purl side, follow these steps:

1. **Slip the first stitch on the LH needle (as if to knit) to the RH needle.**

2. **Do the same to the next stitch.**

3. **Keeping the 2 slipped stitches facing in this direction, transfer them back to the LH needle.**

4. **Purl the 2 stitches together through the back loops (see Figure 6-8).**

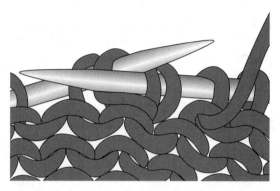

Figure 6-8: Purling 2 slipped stitches through the back of the loops.

Chapter 7

Oops! Fixing Common Mistakes

*A*s a beginning knitter, you may not notice the mistakes in your project, and that's understandable. After all, you're trying to figure out what to do with your hands, the needles, and the yarn, which is quite enough to worry about, thank you very much! After you have the hang of knitting, however, you'll start to notice things — like unusual bumps, unraveling stitches, and strange twists — that don't look quite right.

Take heart — all knitters at all skill levels make mistakes. The trick is to do what you can to reduce the number of mistakes you make, recognize them quickly when you do err, and fix them as soon as you recognize them. This chapter explains how to do all those things.

Stopping Mistakes or Catching Them Early

Some mistakes are minor, such as a dropped or added stitch that you can easily fix (or easily hide). Others are the whoppers of the knitting set — obvious errors that can ruin a project. Because you can't avoid mistakes entirely, your goal should be to make as few mistakes as possible and, when you do flub up, to catch 'em early. Following are suggestions for achieving this goal:

- ✔ **Read the instructions completely and make sure you understand them.** As you read through the pattern instructions row by row, try picturing what's happening. If you're reading a chart, talk yourself through the stitches: "I cast on 98, knit 1, purl 1 for the first 4 rows. Then in the fifth row, I work in stockinette stitch until. . . ."

- ✔ **Practice any stitches, stitch patterns, or techniques you think may trip you up.** Sometimes you can figure out what's going on simply by visualizing the steps. But when you can't picture what's going on — no matter how many times you read the instructions — take a little time to practice with real needles and yarn.

  Checking gauge (see Chapter 3) automatically gives you the opportunity to run through the stitch pattern. If you're one who throws caution to the wind and doesn't check gauge, practice by working up a little swatch with the stitches.

- ✔ **Look at your work.** We know this sounds obvious. But too many knitters get so into the rhythm of actually knitting that they forget to look at their work. Doing so helps you recognize how a particular combination of stitches creates the pattern growing before your eyes. When you recognize that, you're much more aware and able to keep track of the stitches as you work them.

✔ **Count your stitches after each row.** One stitch more or less than you cast on frequently indicates a mistake in the last row you worked.

Dealing with Dropped Stitches

Dropped stitches are stitches that, for one reason or another, fall off the needle and don't get worked. Dropping stitches is pretty common for both beginning and experienced knitters. Sometimes you're lucky enough to recognize the dropped stitch right away; other times you don't notice it until much later. Either way, you need to fix the error because dropped stitches don't look good, and they unravel when the piece is pulled or stretched, leaving an unsightly ladder of yarn up your work.

Some yarns, especially plied ones, are prone to splitting. When you're fixing mistakes (or just knitting in general), take care not to let your needle separate the plies. You want to go in and out of the *holes* in the stitches, leaving the yarn strand intact.

Finding and securing a dropped stitch

When you suspect that you've dropped a stitch, the first thing to do is find it and secure it so that it doesn't unravel any more than it already has. Contrary to knitting lore, a dropped stitch doesn't immediately unravel itself into oblivion — thank goodness! — but you do need to deal with it immediately.

To find a dropped stitch, carefully spread out your stitches along the needle and slowly scan the row(s) below. The telltale sign of a dropped stitch is a horizontal strand of yarn that isn't pulled through a loop. Here's how it may look:

> ✔ **If the dropped stitch hasn't unraveled far, or if you just recently dropped it,** it should look like the one in Figure 7-1. Note the horizontal yarn that didn't get pulled through.

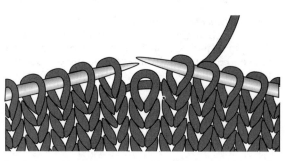

Figure 7-1: A dropped stitch viewed from the knit side.

> ✔ **If the dropped stitch has worked itself down several rows, or if you didn't notice its absence immediately,** it should appear as a wayward stitch at the bottom of a ladder of unworked strands (see Figure 7-2). Each strand represents a row.

When you find the dropped stitch, you need to secure it so that it doesn't unravel any more. To do so, carefully work a small needle tip, the blunt point of a tapestry needle, a toothpick, a nail, a bobby pin, or anything into it to secure it and stretch it out a bit. Then use a safety pin to secure the stitch.

Figure 7-2: A dropped knit stitch and ladder.

Now take a deep breath and follow the instructions in the following sections for getting that dropped stitch back on the needle.

Rescuing a dropped stitch in the row below

After you pin the dropped stitch to secure it (refer to the preceding section), continue working the row above until you reach the pinned stitch directly below. Fortunately, rescuing a stitch dropped in the row below is a simple matter. Basically, you just need to pick up the unworked horizontal strand of yarn behind the stitch and pull it through the dropped stitch. How you go about it depends on whether you want to make a knit stitch or a purl stitch.

To make a knit stitch

If the knit side of your work is facing, rescue the stitch as follows:

1. **Insert your RH needle into the *front* of the dropped stitch.**

   Look behind the stitch. You'll see the horizontal strand of yarn that didn't get pulled through.

2. **With the RH needle, go under the unworked strand from the front (see Figure 7-3).**

   Both the strand and the stitch are on the RH needle.

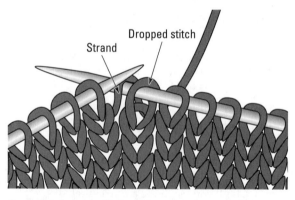

Dropped stitch

Strand

Figure 7-3: A dropped knit stitch ready to be worked.

3. **Insert the LH needle into the stitch from the back (see Figure 7-4) and pull it over the strand.**

   You've just "worked" the stitch that was dropped in the last row. Now you need to knit the stitch in the current row, as the next step describes.

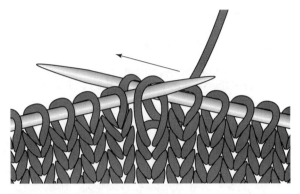

Figure 7-4: Insert the LH needle into the dropped stitch.

4. **Put the new stitch on the LH needle in the ready-to-knit position (see Figure 7-5) and knit as normal.**

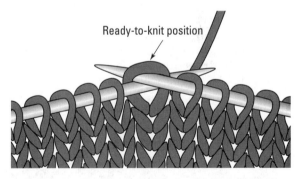

Ready-to-knit position

Figure 7-5: Transfer the stitch to the ready-to-knit position.

Check to see that you've made a smooth knitted V stitch.

To make a purl stitch

If the purl side is facing, or if you're working in garter stitch, rescue the dropped stitch as follows:

1. **Insert the RH needle into the dropped stitch *and* the yarn strand from the *back*, as shown in Figure 7-6.**

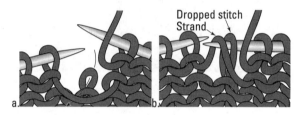

Figure 7-6: Pick up a dropped purl stitch.

   If you can't readily pick up a dropped stitch from the back or front, pick it up any way you can and put it on the RH needle.

2. **Using the LH needle, pull the stitch over the strand and off the needle, forming a new stitch on the RH needle (see Figure 7-7).**

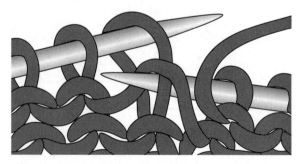

Figure 7-7: Pull the dropped stitch over.

3. **Place the new stitch on the LH needle in the ready-to-work position (see Figure 7-8) and purl (or knit, for a garter stitch) as normal.**

Check to see that you have a bump below the stitch.

Rescuing a dropped stitch from several rows below

Rescuing a dropped stitch that's several rows down is actually pretty easy. All you need is a crochet hook and to know whether to draw the unworked strand through the dropped stitch from the front or the back — and that depends on whether you're working with a stockinette stitch or a garter stitch.

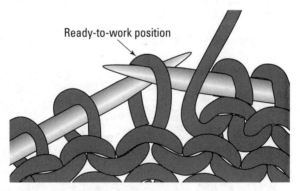

Ready-to-work position

Figure 7-8: Replace the rescued stitch in the ready-to-work position.

In stockinette stitch

To rescue a dropped stitch from the knit side of stockinette stitch (if the purl side is facing, turn it around), reach through the dropped stitch with a crochet hook, and pick up the bottommost strand in the ladder (see Figure 7-9). Then pull the strand through the stitch toward you to form a new stitch. Repeat this maneuver to pull each successive strand in the ladder through the loop until the last strand has been worked.

In garter stitch

To pick up several rows of dropped stitches in garter stitch, you have to alternate the direction from which you pull the ladder strands through the dropped stitch. Pull through the front of the stitch to create a knit stitch, and pull through the back of the stitch for a purl.

To determine whether you pull through the front or back of the stitch, follow the bottom strand to the side (either way) to see what the stitch connected to it looks like. A stitch that looks like a V is a knit stitch; one that looks like a bump is a purl stitch. (Pull gently on the strand to locate the neighboring stitches if you need to.) You can see the connected stitches in Figure 7-10.

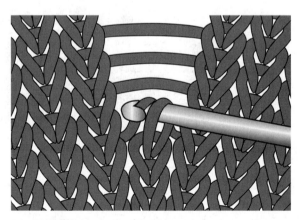

Figure 7-9: Pull through the first strand.

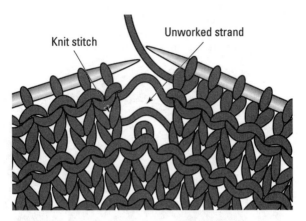

Knit stitch

Unworked strand

Figure 7-10: Knit stitches connected to the strand.

When you know whether the first stitch to be rescued is a knit or purl stitch, the fix is a cinch.

1. **Fix the first stitch.**

   If it's a knit stitch (it looks like a V), pick up the dropped stitch from the front. Refer to the preceding section and Figure 7-9 for detailed instructions. If it's a purl stitch, pick it up from the back, as shown in Figure 7-11.

2. **Alternate pulling stitches from each direction until you've pulled through the last strand.**

   If you fixed the first stitch by pulling the strand through the front, fix the next stitch by pulling the strand through the back, and so on.

3. **Put the last loop onto the LH needle in the ready-to-work position and work it as normal.**

 If you pull a loop through from a strand in the wrong row, you'll have a major — and unsightly — glitch in your work. So, pick up the strands of yarn in the proper order, and check to make sure that the stitch you've made matches the ones next to it.

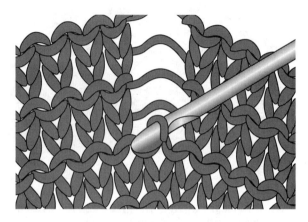

Figure 7-11: Pick up a dropped purl stitch from the back.

Ripping (Your Heart) Out

All sorts of mistakes require that you rip out your knitting. What are they? Inadvertently adding stitches and any other mistake that requires reknitting to fix. How far you have to go depends on the mistake, though. Adding a stitch in the row you're knitting is a relatively painless fix; finding out that you've been knitting the right side stitches on the wrong side of the piece is a bit more cringe-inducing.

If ripping out your work sounds too stressful or like too much work, there are some alternatives for when perfection doesn't matter, no one will know that a mistake has been made (one added stitch in a large afghan, for example), or you don't want to take the time to redo work you've already completed. Here are your options:

- ✔ **Don't do anything.** If you can happily live with imperfections and the mistake doesn't bother you, let it go and keep on knitting.

- ✔ **When the mistake is a simple added stitch (or two), decrease the same number of stitches in the row you're currently working.** Use one of the decreasing techniques in Chapter 6. This is a good alternative when having the extra stitch messes up the pattern and working around it in each row is a hassle.

If the thought of ripping out your knitting is making you a little sick to your stomach, take a minute to laugh at knitting shorthand that online knitters use to refer to ripping out their work: *frog* or *frogging* and *tink*. *Tink* is *knit* spelled backwards, indicating you're doing the reverse. Why *frogging?* Because you need to rip it, rip it.

Ripping out stitch by stitch

If you're lucky enough to catch your mistake before the end of the row in which you made it, you can rip back to your mistake one stitch at a time. Basically, you undo what you've just done until you get to the problem spot. Here's how:

1. **With the knit or purl side facing, insert the LH needle from *front to back* (away from you) into the stitch below the one on the RH needle.**

   Figure 7-12 shows how this looks when you undo a knit stitch or a purl stitch.

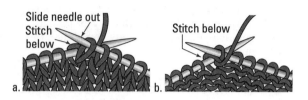

Figure 7-12: Unforming a knit stitch (a) and a purl stitch (b).

2. **Slide the RH needle out of the stitch and gently pull on the yarn to free it.**

   Your work won't unravel because your LH needle has secured the stitch below.

3. **Repeat Steps 1 and 2, stitch by stitch, to the point of your mistake.**

Ripping out row by row

What's the worst-case scenario? You notice a mistake several rows down in your work — a bump or glitch that can't be rescued easily by backing up a few stitches. In such a situation, ripping back one stitch at a time may take longer than simply taking the piece off the needles, undoing your work as far back as necessary, and then starting over. It's a pain. It's no fun. And you'll mourn the time (and possibly inches) of finished work you lose, but sometimes ripping everything out is necessary. When it is, take a deep breath and follow these steps:

1. **Locate the row your mistake is on and mark it with a safety pin.**

2. **Slide your needle out of the stitches.**

   This is where you probably want to take a few deep, steadying breaths.

3. **Pull gently on the working yarn, undoing the stitches.** When you reach the row above the mistake (which you've marked with a safety pin), slowly rip to the end of the row.

4. **Place your knitting so that the working yarn is on the right (flip the fabric over if you have to).**

5. **Insert the tip of the needle into the first stitch on the row below (from back to front, toward you; see Figure 7-13), and gently pull to free the yarn from the stitch.**

   You should have one stitch solidly planted on the RH needle.

 Using a needle several sizes smaller to pick up the last row of your ripped-out knitting makes it easier to snag the stitches. Then, when it's time to begin knitting again, work the next row with your regular needle.

6. **Repeat Step 5 until you reach your mistake.**

   Figure 7-14 shows what it looks like as you work across the row to your mistake.

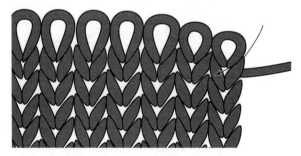

Figure 7-13: Insert the needle into the stitch below.

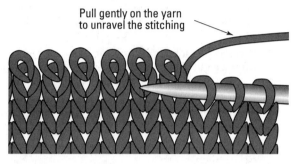

Pull gently on the yarn
to unravel the stitching

Figure 7-14: Put stitches on your RH needle as you work
toward your mistake.

7. **Rip out your mistake, turn your work, and start
   knitting again!**

Chapter 8

Knitting in the Round

● ●

In This Chapter

▶ Selecting circular and double-pointed needles

▶ Discovering how to cast on in circular knitting

▶ Getting started by joining and working basic stitches

▶ Figuring out your gauge

● ●

Knitting in the round, in which you knit around and around on a circular needle to create a seamless tube, is deceptively simple, and many knitters of all skill levels prefer it to flat knitting. Why? For a variety of reasons, but the two most common reasons for beginners are

> ✔ Knitting proceeds faster because you don't have to turn your work.
>
> ✔ You can create stockinette stitch — a common stitch in many beginner and intermediate patterns — without having to purl.

More advanced knitters, especially those who make garments (sweaters, socks, gloves, and so on), like knitting in the round because it cuts down on garment assembly. For these reasons, circular knitting is growing in popularity, and many books for beginning knitters include knit-in-the-round patterns.

This chapter explains everything you need to know to successfully knit in the round. For projects that use this technique, head to Chapter 9.

How Going in Circles Can Be a Good Thing

When you knit in the round (often called *circular knitting*), you work on a circular needle or double-pointed needles (dpns) to knit a seamless tube. Years ago, circular knitting was a technique associated with more-experienced knitters. These days many popular patterns for beginners are written in the round. Many knitters — beginner and advanced — prefer knitting in the round because of its benefits, which include the following:

- ✔ **The right side always faces you.** If you're averse to purling for some reason, knitting in the round allows you to skip it entirely — as long as you stick to stockinette stitch. Having the right side face you also makes working repeating color patterns easier because your pattern is always front and center; you're never looking at the back and having to flip to the front to double-check what color the next stitch should be.

- ✔ **Although circular knitting is great for sweater bodies, sleeves, hats, socks, and mittens, you're not limited to creating tubes.** By using something called a *steek* — a means of opening the tube of knitted fabric with a line of crocheted or machine-sewn stitches — you also can create a flat piece after the fact. And that's good for such things as cardigans.

- ✔ **You can reduce the amount of sewing required for garments.** When you knit back and forth on straight needles, you make flat pieces that have to be sewn together. Circular knitting eliminates many of these seams. In fact, some patterns let you make an entire sweater from bottom to top (or top to bottom) without having a single seam to sew up when the last stitch has been bound off.

Choosing Needles for Circular Knitting

Circular and double-pointed needles are designed for knitting in the round and, as Chapter 2 explains, come in the same sizes as regular knitting needles. When you select circular or double-pointed needles for your projects, keep in mind the tips in this section.

Circular needles

The needle length you choose for your project must be a smaller circumference than the tube you plan to knit; otherwise, you won't be able to comfortably stretch your stitches around the needle. For example, to knit a hat that measures 21 inches around, you need a 16-inch needle because 21 inches worth of stitches won't stretch around 24 inches of needle (which is the next size up from a 16-inch needle). We know it sounds counterintuitive to need a needle smaller in circumference than the knitted project, but the problem is that, because there's no break — no first stitch or last stitch (after all you're knitting a tube) — you can only stretch the fabric as far as you can stretch any two stitches. A 21-inch circular project won't knit comfortably on a 24-inch circular needle because you can't easily stretch 2 stitches 3 inches apart.

 When you first take a circular needle from its package, it will be tightly coiled. Run the coil under hot water or immerse it in a sink of hot water for a few moments to relax the kinks. You can even hang it around the back of your neck while you get your yarn ready; your body heat will help unkink the needle.

Double-pointed needles

Lengths vary from 5 to 10 inches. The shorter ones are great for socks and mittens, and the longer ones work well for hats and sleeves. Aim for 1 inch or so of empty needle at each end. If you leave more than 1 inch, you'll spend too much time sliding stitches down to the tip so that you can knit them; if you leave less than 1 inch, you'll lose stitches off the ends.

If you've never used double-pointed needles before, choose wooden or bamboo ones. Their slight grip on the stitches will keep the ones on the waiting needles from sliding off into oblivion when you're not looking.

Casting On for Circular Knitting

To knit on a circular needle, cast your stitches directly onto the needle as you would on a straight needle. (For a refresher on how to cast on, see Chapter 4.) Here's the important bit: Before you start to knit, *make sure that the cast-on edge isn't twisted around the needle.* If you have stitches that spiral around the needle, you'll feel like a cat chasing its tail when it comes time to find the bottom edge. The yarn end should be coming from the RH needle tip, as shown in Figure 8-1.

Casting on and getting started on a set of double-pointed needles can be a little trickier than using single-pointed needles. Instead of trying to cast all your stitches onto one small needle (which increases the likelihood that some will slip off the other end) or several separate needles (which leaves needles dangling and extra yarn at each needle change), cast the total number of stitches needed onto a single-pointed straight needle of the correct size. Then slip them purlwise onto your double-pointed needles, distributing them in equal or close-to-equal amounts and making sure that the stitches aren't twisted around any of the needles. Leave one of the needles free to start knitting.

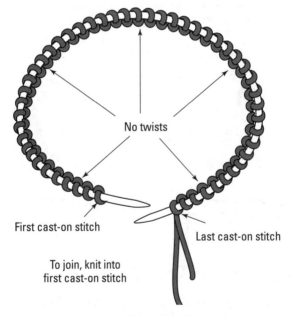

No twists

First cast-on stitch

Last cast-on stitch

To join, knit into
first cast-on stitch

Figure 8-1: Ready to knit on a circular needle.

If you're using a set of four double-pointed needles, use three needles for your stitches: Form them into a triangle (see Figure 8-2a) with the yarn end at the bottom point. Save the fourth (empty) needle for knitting. If you're using a set of five needles, put your stitches on four needles, as shown in Figure 8-2b, and knit with the fifth (empty) needle.

Trying to focus on one of your double-pointed needles while the others are flopping around is pretty frustrating. If you lay your work on a table while transferring your cast-on stitches and arranging your needles, you can keep things steady *and* pay attention to what you're doing at the same time.

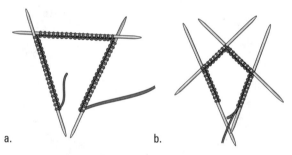

a.   b.

Figure 8-2: Dividing stitches among three (a) and four (b) double-pointed needles.

Joining the Round

Whether you're knitting in the round on a circular or double-pointed needles, after you cast on, pattern instructions tell you to join and begin knitting. *Joining* simply means that when you work the first stitch, you bring the first and last cast-on stitches together, joining the circle of stitches.

Joining on a circular needle

To work the first stitch of the round, follow these steps:

1. **Place a marker on the RH needle before making the first stitch if you want to keep track of the beginning of the round.**

   Many in-the-round patterns tell you to place a marker to indicate the beginning of a round. When you're doing color work or any sort of repeating pattern, knowing where one round ends and another begins is vital. And if you have to place other markers later (common with pieces that require shaping), do something to differentiate your "beginning" marker from the others: Make it a different color than the other markers you use, or attach a piece of yarn or a safety pin to it.

2. **Insert the tip of the RH needle into the first stitch on the LH needle (the first cast-on stitch) and knit or purl as usual.**

   Figure 8-3 shows the first stitch being made with a marker in place.

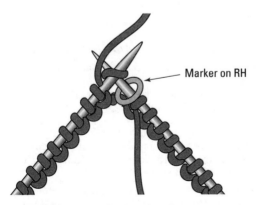

Marker on RH

Figure 8-3: The first stitch in a round.

Joining on double-pointed needles

For double-pointed needles, use the empty needle to begin working the first round. If the first stitch is a knit stitch, make sure that the yarn is in back of your work. If the first stitch is a purl stitch, bring the yarn to the front between the needles, bring the empty needle *under* the yarn, and insert it to purl into the first stitch on the LH needle. After the first couple of stitches, arrange the back ends of the two working needles on top of the other needles. (Do you feel like you have a spider by one leg?) The first round or two may feel awkward, but as your piece begins to grow, the weight of your knitting will keep the needles nicely in place and you'll cruise along.

When you knit on double-pointed needles, the stitches worked where the needles meet may be looser than the rest. To keep them neat, give an extra tug on the yarn as you work the first stitch on each needle and remember to tug again after you insert the needle into the second stitch. Or, when you come to the end of a needle, knit the first stitch or two from the next one before switching to the empty needle.

Tidying up the first and last stitches

Whether you're working on a circular needle or double-pointed needles, the first and last cast-on stitches rarely make a neat join. To tighten up the connection, you can do one of the following:

✔ Cast on an extra stitch at the end, transfer it to the LH needle, and make your first stitch a k2tog, working the increased stitch with the first stitch on the LH needle.

✔ Before working the first stitch, wrap the yarn around the first and last cast-on stitches as follows:

1. Transfer the first stitch on the LH needle to the RH needle.

2. Take the ball yarn from front to back between the needles, and transfer the first 2 stitches on the RH needle to the LH needle.

3. Bring the yarn forward between the needles, and transfer the first stitch on the LH needle back to the RH needle.

4. Take the yarn to the back between the stitches, and give a little tug on the yarn.

You're ready to knit the first stitch.

Working Common Stitches in the Round

When knitting in the round, the right side is always facing you — which is a good thing as long as you understand how it affects the stitches you make. For example, whereas in flat knitting you create a garter stitch by knitting every row, knitting every round in circular knitting produces stockinette stitch.

So, here's a quick guide to getting the stitches you want:

✔ **For garter stitch:** Alternate a knit round with a purl round.

✔ **For stockinette stitch:** Knit all rounds.

✔ **For rib stitches:** In round 1, alternate knit and purl stitches in whatever configuration you choose (1 x 1, 2 x 2, and so on). In subsequent rounds, knit over the knit stitches and purl over the purl stitches.

The trick is simply knowing how the stitch is created in flat knitting and then remembering the principle. For example, in seed stitch you knit in the purl stitches and purl in the knit stitches. Well, you do the same in circular knitting.

Using Steeks for a Clean Break

Steeks are an excellent way to open up a knitted tube. Traditionally, Nordic-style ski sweaters were knit in the round and then steeked to open the cardigan front and sleeve openings. You can use steeks for this type of project or anywhere else you'd like to cut open a line of knit stitches.

You can steek with a sewing machine or a crochet hook, depending on your comfort level with either and whether you have access to a machine. Crocheted steeks are generally simpler to work with for beginners because they're easy to tear out if you make a mistake.

Sewing in a steek

To make a steek with a sewing machine, sew two vertical lines of stitches an inch or so apart (see Figure 8-4). Be sure to keep the line of machine stitching between the same two columns of knit stitches all the way down. Use a sturdy cotton/poly blend thread and a stitch length appropriate to the knitted stitches (shorter for finer-gauge knits, slightly longer for chunkier knits).

Crocheting a steek

To make a steek with yarn, crochet two vertical columns of stitches an inch or more apart using a slip stitch (see

Figure 8-5). Fold the sweater at the line you plan to
stitch so the vertical column of stitches looks like the
top of a crochet chain, then insert your hook into the
first V, yarn over the hook, pull the new loop through
the V, and move to the next stitch on your left, repeating
as you go. Be sure to work only your crocheted stitches
on the same column of knit stitches; if you veer to the
left or right, your steek will be crooked.

Cutting your fabric after you steek

After you've sewn or crocheted the steek in place, it's
safe to cut your knitted fabric between the two lines
of stitching, as shown in Figure 8-6. Then you can
continue with your pattern as directed.

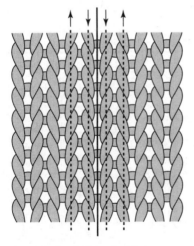

Figure 8-4: Sew two vertical lines.

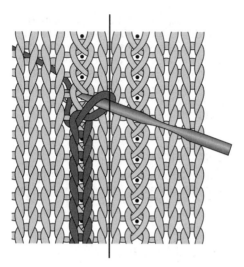

Figure 8-5: Crocheting a steek in place.

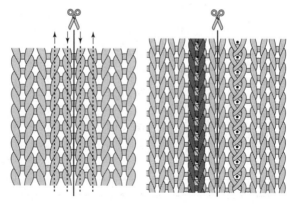

Figure 8-6: Cut between the two lines to open the fabric.

Measuring Gauge in the Round

Knitting stockinette stitch in the round can give you a
different gauge than if you were knitting the same
stitch flat (back and forth on straight needles). Here's
why: A purl stitch is very slightly larger than a knit
stitch. When you work stockinette stitch on straight
needles, every other row is a purl row, and the difference in the sizes of your knits and purls averages out.
However, when working stockinette stitch in the
round, you always make *knit* stitches, which can
result in a slightly smaller piece even though you're
knitting the same pattern over the same number of
stitches. (See Chapter 3 for more on gauge.)

When the gauge for a project worked on a circular
needle must be exact, make your gauge swatch by
working all the rows from the right side, as follows:

1. **Using the same needle you plan to use in
   your project, cast on 24 stitches or so and work
   1 row.**

   Don't turn the work.

2. **Cut the yarn and slide your knitting, with the
   right side facing, back to the knitting end of the
   needle.**

3. **Knit another row, and cut the yarn.**

4. **Repeat Steps 2 and 3 until you've completed
   your swatch, and then measure your gauge.**

An easier and less time-consuming way to measure gauge in circular patterns is to do it while
you knit the piece. Knit at least 1½ inches in the
round on the needles you plan to use, stop, and
measure the stitch gauge and 1-inch of row
gauge. If your gauge is too big, switch to smaller

needles on the next round; if your gauge is too small, switch to bigger needles. If your gauge is off by more than a stitch, tear out the stitches you just made and start again.

Chapter 9

Practicing with Simple Projects

• •

In This Chapter
▶ Creating bags that you can take everywhere
▶ Playing around with a pillow pattern
▶ Knitting a scarf to warm your neck all winter long
▶ Keeping your head cozy in a homemade knitted hat

• •

Knitting swatches is fun for a while, but the point of knitting is to make things that you can use — or that you can give as gifts to the people you care about. The projects in this chapter let you practice working the basic knit stitches, reading and understanding patterns for knitted garments, and, if you decide to give them your own dimensions, working with gauge. *And* you end up with something that you can use yourself or give to friends and family.

You can use the yarn we specify for each project, another yarn with a similar stitch gauge, or a yarn with the generic yarn gauge or weight given. Because this is just practice, don't be overly concerned about matching gauge. It's not a catastrophe if these projects turn out an inch bigger or smaller. Just knit until the piece you're working on measures the length given in the pattern.

Everywhere Bag in Garter Stitch

This basic bag (shown in Figure 9-1) is handy for carrying your wallet, keys, and some lip balm. Make it larger and throw in your glasses case and a notebook. Make it even bigger, add a pocket, and use it for a knitting bag. You can find several ways to vary this project at the end of this section. So, cast on and get started!

Materials and vital statistics

- ✔ **Measurements:** 8 inches x 9 inches, with a 4-inch flap
- ✔ **Yarn:** Tahki Donegal Tweed (100% wool); 3.5 ounces; 1 skein; any color
- ✔ **Needles:** One pair of size US 7 (4½ mm) needles
- ✔ **Other materials:** One button, any size
- ✔ **Gauge:** 18 stitches per 4 inches in garter stitch (4½ stitches per 1 inch)

Directions

All you need to do to make this versatile bag is knit a rectangle, sew up the sides, make and attach a cord for the strap, make a button loop, and attach a button. *Voilà!*

Knitting the bag

Cast on 38 sts.

Work in garter stitch until the piece measures 22 inches in length. (***Remember:*** In garter stitch, you never have to purl; just knit every row.)

Bind off and steam lightly.

Figure 9-1: Everywhere Bag.

Sewing the side seams

Measure down 9 inches from one edge and fold your piece with wrong sides together.

Even though garter stitch is reversible, your cast-on edge looks different from each side. Choose the side you like better and make that side the right side.

Sew the sides closed. You should have 4 inches left over for the flap. It doesn't really matter how you sew the sides closed, but to make a neat seam, use a tapestry needle and a strand of the same yarn.

Making and attaching the cord strap

You can make cords in a variety of ways. Following is a good method to get you started.

Cast on 189 sts (about 42 inches of stitches).

Work in garter stitch for 3 rows.

Bind off.

Using the same yarn you used for the bag, sew the ends of the strap to either side of the top of the bag.

Forming the button loop and attaching the button

You can make a small button loop just as you would make the cord strap — just make it shorter.

Cast on 8 sts.

Knit 1 row.

Bind off.

To attach the button loop to the bag, center the loop on the bag flap with the ends 1 inch or so apart, and attach it with yarn. Using embroidery floss or sewing thread, sew your button on the bag, making sure it's opposite the loop on the flap.

If you work the bag in a plied yarn, you can separate a single ply and use that to sew on your
button. Then the "thread" matches your bag
exactly!

Variations

You can alter this basic bag in a number of ways. By
changing the stitch, making a different cord or closure,
or felting it, you can create entirely different bags.

Use a different stitch pattern

You don't have to knit this bag in garter stitch. Instead,
try stockinette stitch, a combination of garter stitch
and stockinette stitch, or any of the stitch patterns presented in Chapter 5. Remember that textured pattern
stitches show up better in a smooth-plied yarn.

 Consider knitting your project in one stitch pattern and then knitting a pocket for it in a different stitch pattern.

Substituting one stitch
pattern for another

If you decide to substitute a different knit/purl pattern for
garter or stockinette stitch in any of the projects in this
chapter, don't start knitting until you've mapped out how the
pattern will be centered on your project piece. You want to be
sure that your pattern will come out symmetrically. Use graph
paper and plot your pattern by using knit and purl symbols to
see that it begins and ends symmetrically. Remember, to be
symmetrical, a pattern with a single center stitch needs to go
on an uneven number of stitches, and a pattern with 2 center
stitches needs to go on an even number of stitches.

Elizabeth Zimmerman and her idiot cord (I-cord)

Elizabeth Zimmerman, author of *Knitting Without Tears* (Simon & Schuster), was the first person to bring her simple method for working a cord to knitters' attention and give it the name *idiot cord* (or *I-cord*). Her books are an indispensable part of any knitter's library. Zimmerman's "unvented" techniques and her novel way of thinking about knitting and designing have converted many halfhearted knitters into knitting enthusiasts.

Follow these steps to make your very own I-cord:

1. **Using double-pointed needles the same size as or one size smaller than the one you used for your project, cast on 4 stitches.**

2. **Knit the 4 stitches.**

3. **Instead of turning your work, slide the stitches you just worked to the opposite end of the needle, right side still facing.**

4. **With the yarn end at the *left* end of your work, knit another row, pulling slightly on the yarn after you make the first stitch.**

5. **Continue knitting a row and then sliding the stitches to the opposite end of the needle in order to knit them again until your cord is as long as you want it.**

When you're done, you'll have created a cord that curls in on itself.

Warning: Be careful not to let your stitches slide off the end of your needle. Trying to get them back on in the proper order is a real bear; if you don't get them right, you end up with twisted stitches and a sloppy looking cord. Many a knitter has ended up ripping out the entire cord and starting over just to avoid the headache.

Try a different cord

To make a tubelike cord, cast on 4 stitches, knit Row 1
(RS), and purl Row 2. Repeat these rows until the cord
measures 44 inches (or as long as you'd like it to be).
Because stockinette fabric rolls to the wrong side, the
strip will form a tube and you won't need to seam it.

For a closed tube cord, you can work a cord in the
round on two double-pointed needles. Cast on 4
stitches and follow the instructions for making I-cord
in the sidebar "Elizabeth Zimmerman and her idiot
cord (I-cord)." Use a needle the same size or one size
smaller than you used in your bag.

Make a different closure

For the tubelike button loop, cast on 2 or 3 stitches,
work in stockinette stitch for 2 inches, and then bind
off. Center the loop on the bag flap with the ends 1
inch or so apart, and sew on with yarn.

Embellish your bag

Work embroidery on your bag before stitching it up.
Add beads, fringe, or tassels.

Make a pillow instead of a bag

Cast on 63 stitches. Work in garter or stockinette stitch
until the piece measures 16 inches from the beginning.

Join a second color and continue working in garter
stitch until the piece measures 15 inches from the
color change.

Bind off.

Fold the piece so that the two edges overlap in the
center of the work by 2 inches.

Sew the side seams together.

To make button loops, cast on 2 stitches and work in St st until the piece measures 2¼ inches. Cast off.

Fold the loops in half and sew the ends of the button loops evenly spaced along the overlapping edge of the pillow.

Sew buttons under the button loops or buttonholes, and button up!

Make or buy a 14-x-14-inch fabric pillow form for the inside of the pillow.

Felting the bag

Felting knitted fabric makes it much more dense, so there's less chance that your lip gloss or keys will poke through the stitches if you have a tendency to fill up your purse! You felt knitted fabric by putting it into your washer on a hot wash/cold rinse cycle. Yes, hot then cold! You're deliberately shrinking it, so don't put any good sweaters in the same load.

Felted knits lose more length than width when they shrink. To keep a felted bag the same dimensions as its knit-only counterpart, you need to knit about one-third more rows . . . sometimes even more, depending on the yarn. So, if you're supposed to knit the bag piece 22 inches long, you should knit about 28 to 29 inches instead. It should shrink only a little bit width-wise, but to be safe, add an extra 5 stitches to the cast-on width.

 If you seam the sides with yarn before you felt the bag, the sides will be stronger than if you sew them together afterward. And if you want a felted strap, don't attach it before felting the rest of the bag — put it in to shrink unattached. Straps can get caught on the center agitator of your washing machine and pull out of shape very easily.

Throw Pillow

Pillows, like the ones shown in Figure 9-2, are semiquick knits with a lot of variations — and they look great on your favorite chair or couch!

Figure 9-2: Throw Pillow.

Materials and vital statistics

- ✔ **Measurements:** Vary depending on yarn weight and needle size
- ✔ **Yarn:** Approximately 400 yards of yarn for a standard 14-x-14-inch pillow form (see directions on the pillow form for information on making covers in different sizes)
- ✔ **Needles:** One pair in a size appropriate for the yarn selected (check its ball band if you're not sure); yarn needle for seaming
- ✔ **Other materials:** One 14-x-14-inch pillow form; one to three (or more!) large decorative buttons
- ✔ **Gauge:** Varies depending on yarn weight and needle size

Directions

Cast on your gauge per inch times 14 (the pillow form's width), plus 4 extra stitches to allow for easy seaming on either side. So, if your yarn is 4 stitches to the inch and you're making a 14-inch-wide pillow, cast on 60 stitches ([4 × 14] + 4).

Knit until the piece measures two times your pillow's height, plus 4 inches.

Bind off and block.

Finishing: Fold the bottom of the piece up until you have a 14-x-14-inch square, and seam the sides. Create your loop closures. As in the Everywhere Bag pattern, you can knit a wide variety of loop closures. Fold the 4-inch flap over the top and stitch your chosen buttons into place evenly below the bottom edge of the flap. Knit loop closures long enough to reach around each button, and sew them into place. Insert your pillow form, and you're done!

Variations

Knit six 4-inch pieces of I-cord, and sew three of them evenly across the bottom of the fold-over flap. Sew the other three in corresponding positions on the body of the bag, and tie it up.

To make a nice flat fold line at the bottom and top edges of the pillow, when your piece measures 14 inches long (or a perfect square for your chosen pillow form size), purl 1 RS row of stitches if you're knitting in stockinette or 3 rows of stockinette if you're knitting in garter stitch. Repeat after you knit another 14 inches or the height of your pillow.

In-the-Round Projects

When you think of in-the-round projects, you may think of socks and mittens — things that obviously use tube shapes — but in-the-round knitting has broadened beyond the basics. This section includes three in-the-round projects for beginners: a scarf, a bag, and a hat.

Natasha Scarf

Are you impatient? Then the Natasha Scarf (shown in Figure 9-3) is the scarf pattern for you. Using super-ultra-chunky yarn and large needles, you can make one of these scarves in less than an hour if you concentrate.

If you make this scarf a little on the tight side, it makes a great ski headband.

Figure 9-3: Natasha Scarf.

Materials and vital statistics

- ✔ **Measurements:** 18 inches in diameter x 6 inches
- ✔ **Yarn:** Ultra-chunky yarn; 50 yards

  Brown Sheep Burly Spun is a good choice of yarn, or if your local yarn store stocks spinning supplies, you can also knit this scarf from unspun spinning fiber.
- ✔ **Needles:** One pair of size US 13 (8 mm) or 15 (9 mm) needles
- ✔ **Gauge:** Unimportant. As knitted here from unspun spinning fiber, the gauge is approximately 1 stitch per 1 inch.

Directions

Cast on 8 sts and knit, wrapping yarn around your needle twice. When you knit the next row, the extra wrap will drop from your needle and make the row twice as high as it would normally be. Continue knitting this way until the piece measures 15 to 17 inches (or large enough to wrap around your neck snugly, but not too tightly).

Bind off and seam the ends together.

Modified Messenger Bag

What makes a messenger bag a messenger bag? A sizeable front flap, but this modified messenger bag (shown in Figure 9-4) has a smaller flap along with a charming I-cord buttonhole loop. Tired of boring bag straps? The "Variations" section has plenty of ideas for you to play around with.

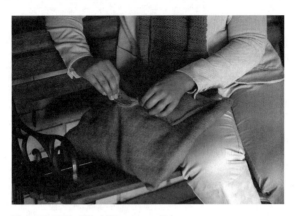

Figure 9-4: Modified Messenger Bag.

Materials and vital statistics

- ✔ **Measurements:** 20 inches x 15 inches

- ✔ **Yarn:** Heavy worsted-weight wool; approximately 450 yards

- ✔ **Needles:** One 24-inch size US 10 (6 mm) F; two size US 10 dpns; yarn or tapestry needle for weaving in ends

- ✔ **Other materials:** One large button or toggle closure; strap of your choice (see "Variations" section); coordinating sewing thread and needle

- ✔ **Gauge:** 4 stitches and 6 rows per 1 inch

Directions

Using a size US 10 circular needle, cast on 150 sts and join round, being careful not to twist the stitches.

Knit for 14 inches, and then bind off 100 sts.

Knit for 5 inches, and then bind off 23 sts.

Slip next 4 sts onto one dpn, and knit 3 inches of I-cord or enough to go around your button of choice to allow easy buttoning and unbuttoning.

Bind off 3 sts, and place the last st onto the needle with the remaining 22 sts (23 sts).

Bind off.

Finishing: Seam bottom of bag closed, and weave in all ends. Sew on strap and/or button(s).

Variations

You can modify your messenger bag in a variety of ways. Following are some suggestions:

- ✔ Knit the bag for 20 inches instead of 14, and then felt it.

- ✔ Experiment with unusual straps to make your bag stand out. Options include multiple strands of knitted I-cord that you braid together or even a braided fabric tube strap (to match a fabric lining for the bag, perhaps?). Search thrift stores or the back of your closet for interesting old belts, which make great straps — and very sturdy ones, to boot. (Of course, you can always opt for nylon webbing, sold in sewing stores.)

- ✔ Knit buttonholes into the bottom edge of your bag's flap instead of using a buttonhole loop.

- ✔ Make your bag from stripes of various leftover yarns. Better still, get together with your knitting friends and swap leftover yarns; even if you all knit the same pattern, your bags will look quite different.

Ribbed Watchman's Cap

This classically masculine hat (shown in Figure 9-5) looks great on women, too — just choose a bright color, or trim it with a knitted flower. Patterned yarn such as a handpainted, multishade colorway will be broken up by the 3-stitch rib, which is an interesting visual effect.

Adult human heads are about the same size (give or take a little), and knitted in the round with some decreases at the top, this hat will fit no matter what yarn you use.

 A good way to make sure a hat will fit you is to try it on after you've knit 1 or 2 inches. Rip out the existing stitches and move up or down a needle size if the hat is a little too small or big.

Materials and vital statistics

- **Measurements:** 21 inches in diameter x 7½ inches

- **Yarn:** Worsted-weight wool; 125 yards

- **Needles:** One 16-inch size US 9 (5½ mm) circular needle; four or five size US 9 dpns; yarn or tapestry needle

- **Gauge:** 4 stitches and 6 rows per 1 inch

Directions

Cast on 84 sts.

* K3, p3; rep from * until piece measures 6 inches.

Begin decreases:

Round 1: * P1, p2tog, k3; rep from * to end of round (70 sts).

Round 2: * P2, k3; rep from * to end of round.

Round 3: * P2, k1, k2tog; rep from * to end of round (56 sts).

Round 4: * P2, k2; rep from * to end of round.

Round 5: * P2tog, k2; rep from * to end of round (42 sts).

Round 6: * P1, k2; rep from * to end of round.

Round 7: * P1, k2tog; rep from * to end of round (28 sts). Switch to the double-pointed needles, dividing stitches evenly.

Round 8: * P1, k1; rep from * to end of round.

Round 9: * K2tog; rep from * to end of round (14 sts).

Round 10: * K2tog; rep from * to end of round (7 sts).

Cut yarn, leaving at least a 12-inch tail.

Finishing: Thread tail onto yarn needle, and then slip remaining stitches onto yarn needle. Pull opening closed, push yarn tail to reverse side of fabric, and weave in ends.

Figure 9-5: Ribbed Watchman's Cap.